Unconditional Surrender

Karl Dönitz in the witness box at the International Military Tribunal, Nuremberg, 1946.

Unconditional Surrender

A Memoir of the Last Days of the Third Reich and the Dönitz Administration

Walter Lüdde-Neurath

Foreword by Jürgen Rohwer

Translation by Geoffrey Brooks

Frontline Books, London

NAVAL INSTITUTE PRESS
Annapolis, Maryland

This edition published in 2010 by Frontline Books, an imprint of
Pen & Sword Books Ltd., 47 Church Street, Barnsley,
S. Yorkshire, S70 2AS.

Visit us at www.frontline-books.com, email info@frontline-books.com
or write to us at the above address.

Published and distributed in the United States and Canada by the
Naval Institute Press
291 Wood Road, Annapolis, Maryland 21402-5034
www.nip.org

Authorised translation of the German edition, published by
Muster-Schmidt Verlag.

UK edition: ISBN 978-1-84832-568-5
US edition: ISBN 978-1-59114-894-4

PUBLISHING HISTORY
Regierung Dönitz: die letzten Tage des Dritten Reiches was originally published
in 1950 by Muster-Schmidt Verlag (Göttingen). A second edition was released in
1953. In 1964, following the release of new documentary
evidence, a third expanded edition was published with supplementary
material by Professor Walter Baum, which is included in this new
edition. This is the first English-language translation and includes a
new foreword by Jürgen Rohwer and a new plate section.

CIP data records for this title are available from the British Library
and the Library of Congress.

Library of Congress Control Number: 2010927716

Typeset by Mac Style, Beverley, E. Yorkshire
Printed in Great Britain by MPG Books Limited

Contents

List of Illustrations

Frontispiece: Karl Dönitz in the witness box at the International Military Tribunals, Nuremberg, 1946

(plates between pages 78 and 79)

Timetable of Events

16 Dec 1944	The German Ardennes offensive begins.
12 Jan 1945	Major Soviet offensive breaks through the central section of the main German front at Baranov. The German Vistula Front collapses.
7 Mar 1945	The Germans lose the Rhine bridge at Remagen.
15 Apr 1945	Hitler issues his order for the division of the Reich into two parts (Dönitz – North, Kesselring – South).
16 Apr 1945	Major Soviet offensive on the Oder Front.
19 Apr 1945	Soviets break through at Wriezen and Müncheberg. The Battle for Berlin begins.
20 Apr 1945	Dönitz becomes Commander-in-Chief North (Appendix 2). Russian artillery bombards Berlin.
21 Apr 1945	Last meeting between Hitler and Dönitz, who is released to 'defend the northern region'.
22 Apr 1945	Dönitz transfers from Berlin to Plön/Holstein. Hitler resolves to remain in Berlin.
23 Apr 1945	Göring's 'treason': Generalfeldmarschall Ritter von Greim is made Commander-in-Chief Luftwaffe.
24 Apr 1945	OKW (Keitel, Jodl) transfers from Berlin to Rheinsberg. Berlin is surrounded.
25 Apr 1945	Speer's last visit to Hitler: afterwards he returns to Dönitz.
27 Apr 1945	Dönitz, Himmler, Keitel and Jodl meet at Rheinsberg. The effort to relieve Berlin fails.
29 Apr 1945	Hitler signs his Last Will and Testament (Appendix 3).
30 Apr 1945	Early: Bormann's signal about Himmler's 'treason'.

| | 1400 hrs: Dönitz and Himmler arrive in Lübeck. Exchange of telegrams with Gauleiter Kaufmann regarding the capitulation of Hamburg (Appendix 4). |

1400 hrs: Dönitz and Himmler arrive in Lübeck. Exchange of telegrams with Gauleiter Kaufmann regarding the capitulation of Hamburg (Appendix 4).

1530 hrs: Hitler commits suicide.

1835 hrs: Receipt of signal regarding Dönitz's nomination to succeed Hitler (Appendix 5).

1 May 1945   1053 hrs: Signal 'Testament in force' (Appendix 5).

1518 hrs: Signal 'Führer deceased yesterday' (Appendix 5).

Dönitz broadcasts to the nation.

Foreign Minister Ribbentrop dismissed.

2 May 1945   Heeresgruppe Süd-west (Italy) capitulates.

British and US forces reach the Baltic Sea.

Capitulation talks with the Western Powers.

Transfer of HQ to Flensburg.

Reich Government resigns.

3 May 1945   Admiral von Friedeburg negotiates capitulation with Montgomery. Discussions at HQ about the occupied territories.

4 May 1945   Partial capitulation of the German North region, Holland and Denmark is signed (Appendix 12).

U-boat war suspended.

U-boats in German waters are scuttled.

5 May 1945   0800 hrs: Partial capitulation in force.

Werwolf called off.

Von Friedeburg negotiates at Eisenhower's HQ.

Caretaker Reich Government formed under leadership of Reichsminister Graf Schwerin von Krosigk.

6 May 1945   Jodl negotiates at Eisenhower's HQ.

Himmler relieved of all offices.

7 May 1945   0241 hrs: Acceptance of unconditional surrender at Rheims.

1245 hrs: Schwerin von Krosigk broadcasts to the nation (Appendix 19).

8 May 1945	Instrument of capitulation ratified at Berlin-Karlshorst (Appendix 16).
	Dönitz broadcasts to the nation (Appendix 22).
9 May 1945	0001 hrs: The guns fall silent.
11 May 1945	The 'Allied Control Commission at OKW' establishes channels to the Government and OKW.
13 May 1945	Generalfeldmarschall Keitel arrested.
	Generaloberst Jodl heads OKW.
17 May 1945	The Russian Staff of the Control Commission meets in Flensburg.
23 May 1945	The Caretaker Reich Government is disbanded (Appendix 24), its members arrested and taken off to Bad Mondorf, Luxembourg.
5 Jun 1945	Allied declaration of the 'capitulation' of 'Germany' (Appendix 26).

Foreword

Walter Lüdde-Neurath was born on 15 June 1914 at Hüningen, a small village in Alsace. He passed his Abitur from his high grammar school at Görlitz in Eastern Saxonia in 1932. The following year he joined the Reichsmarine as an officer candidate. After training he was commissioned as Leutnant zur See in October 1936. He served mostly in torpedo boats and destroyers. From March 1939 to September 1941 he was torpedo officer on the newly commissioned destroyer *Karl Galster*. From the beginning of the war to the invasion of Norway the *Karl Galster* was involved in laying the 'Westwall' defensive minefields and then several offensive minefields off the east coast of England, and also escorted capital ships during some forays into the northern North Sea and in June/July into the Arctic and the Iceland-Faeroes Passage. In September the *Karl Galster* was transferred first to Cherbourg with other destroyers and then to Brest and participated in mine-laying operations in the Bristol Channel and forays against shipping off the south coast of England. At the end of November there was an action with the British 5th Destroyer Flotilla, in which the destroyer HMS *Javelin* was torpedoed. In December the *Karl Galster* was transferred back to Germany. After some dockyard repairs in June 1941 she escorted the heavy cruiser *Lützow* during her abortive breakout into the Atlantic and in July the destroyer flotilla was transferred to Kirkenes to operate against Soviet shipping in the Eastern Barents Sea.

In September Lüdde-Neurath was transferred to Bremen to be the executive officer of the new destroyer *Z 30*, building at the Deschimag yard, which was commissioned in November 1941. In March 1942 *Z 30* was part of the escort force for the cruiser *Admiral Hipper*'s voyage to Norway, and in July she participated in the short-lived fleet operation against convoy PQ 17. In November 1942 Korvettenkapitän Lüdde-Neurath was sent to be commanding officer of the torpedo boat *Jaguar* operating at the time in the Bay of Biscay escorting blockade runners going out to or returning from Japan. In early 1943 the *Jaguar* returned to Germany and was transferred to escort capital ships to Norway and to participate in laying defensive minefields to lengthen the 'Westwall' barrages. In mid-1943 the *Jaguar* returned to the Bay of Biscay to help protect U-boats on their way out and back from their operating areas against RAF air attacks. In between Lüdde-Neurath acted as a substitute commanding officer aboard the torpedo boats *Möwe* and *Greif.* After a short course at the *Kriegsakademie* from April to June 1944 he took command of the destroyer *Richard Beitzen* and was then transferred to the staff of the Commander of Destroyers.

In September 1944 Lüdde-Neurath was selected by the commander-in-chief of the Kriegsmarine to be his adjutant. During the last months of the war, therefore, he served as adjutant to Grossadmiral Karl Dönitz and came into close contact with him. During the final days of the war in April 1945 he participated in almost all the Grossadmiral's activities, and he was with Dönitz when the radio message came in the afternoon of 30 April appointing him as Hitler's successor. He was party to all the discussions in the days that followed when attempts were made to come to an armistice with the Western Allies and finally also when unconditional surrender was decided upon on 8 May. Dönitz then established a 'government', and Lüdde-Neurath was with him until its dissolution on 23 May 1945.

During all this time Lüdde-Neurath took daily notes about all important events, the meetings with members of the government, and most importantly of his exchanges of views with Dönitz. So he is probably the best eyewitness for Dönitz's intentions and decisions. And because there are almost no publications about the top German decision-makers at this time, it is most welcome that a British publisher has taken the opportunity to publish Lüdde-Neurath's diary along with the documents he collected later on. His book was finished in autumn 1948, so his account of the days from late April to 23 May 1945 is uninfluenced by subsequent opinions. Lüdde-Neurath's book is therefore a primary source for Dönitz's time as commander-in-chief of the navy from autumn 1944 to April 1945 and then for the time of the Dönitz Government.

I was at this time a young Leutnant zur See and became a student of history when Musterschmidt Verlag at Göttingen published the first edition of this work. I was then collecting all materials about the history of the German navy and had come into contact with many former admirals and other officers to interview them about their experiences during the war. In particular, I met Fregattenkapitän Günter Hessler, formerly the senior staff officer with the Commander U-Boats, his father-in-law Karl Dönitz. Hessler was then working on a history of the U-boat War in the Atlantic for the British Admiralty, and I assisted him in collecting all data about attacks and sinkings by the U-boats. During my visits to Hessler's office at Brunsbüttel we had many conversations about his relations to Dönitz and his experiences with him as the commander of the U-boats. Hessler introduced me to Dönitz after his release from Spandau Prison in 1956.

From this time on I visited Dönitz about two to three times a year at Reinbek near Hamburg and we had many discussions about the U-boat War, his ideas on leadership and his dealings with Hitler. During these discussions between 1957 and 1979, and from countless conversations with members of his staff, I got a good impression of Dönitz's leadership methods and of his relationship to Hitler.

In terms of his leadership tactics, his most important priority was to concentrate all his energy and knowledge on the task given, without looking too much into the spheres of other leaders or commanders, especially the army or the air force. It was his principle not to interfere with the competence of other people and to prevent other people interfering with his own sphere of responsibility.

Even more important were his close relations with his subordinates in the 'U-Bootwaffe', which inspired great confidence in his men. When he became commander-in-chief of the navy there were several admirals who were senior to him. He was able to retire some of those who might have given him trouble, but without causing ill feeling. Others he kept in their posts.

It is important to say that he as long as he was Commander U-Boats (BdU, or *Befehlshaber der U-Boote*) he met with Hitler at ceremonies to decorate U-boat commanders. Only when he became commander-in- chief of the navy did this situation change. During some of my visits to Dönitz I asked him about this change. He said that when Raeder had been commander-in-chief he did not have a good relationship with Hitler and avoided meeting him as much as possible. When it became necessary to take problems with the Kriegsmarine to Hitler, Raeder presented his proposals, which Hitler in most cases acknowledged, then Raeder went away, not necessarily ensuring that Hitler's responses were carried through into action. So Dönitz decided that he had to win Hitler's trust and confidence, which was possible only by going to Führer Headquarters relatively frequently – unlike Raeder. So, for example, not long after Raeder's dismissal for his refusal to accept Hitler's orders to scrap the major surface units and use their guns for coastal defence, Dönitz was able to get that order dropped. However, although reciprocal trust and confidence grew at these visits once or twice a month, Dönitz also came under the influence of Hitler's strong personality, in the same way as many of the army generals had done. A member of his staff told me after Dönitz's death: 'When Dönitz came back from the headquarters and his visits to Hitler it always took two or three days before he was "normal" again.'

After the change of the tide in the Battle of the Atlantic in May 1943, Dönitz hoped to resume the campaign again with the 'true' submarine Types XXI and XXIII U-boats he had ordered in September and November 1943 to be completed by mid-1944. The first boats were actually completed in May/June 1944, but the whole building programme was delayed by the Allied air raids. In addition, the training programme for the new boats was affected by developments on the Eastern Front, when the Soviet armies broke through to the Baltic Sea, and the training areas had to be reduced. But when at the end of 1944 sixty-five Type XXI and thirty-one Type XXIII U-boats had been commissioned, he still hoped to resume the U-boat war with some success because the Allied anti-submarine vessels were too slow to catch the new boats. He mentioned this to Hitler, who put some hope into this possibility together with the other new weapons such as the V-1 and V-2 and the jet fighters. (Another good source for the discussions at Führer Headquarters' is *Lagevorträge des Oberbefehlshabers der Kriegsmarine vor Hitler 1939-1945*. Herausgegeben von Gerhard Wagner. München: J.F. Lehmanns Verlag, 1972. Konteradmiral Gerhard Wagner was at the time the 'Admiral z.B.V.'[1] and took part in many conferences with Hitler.)

In January 1945 the Red Army began its great offensive, encircling Army Group Kurland and the city of Memel as well as driving apart German forces in East Prussia and Pomerania, where the troops were forced into cramped pockets on the coast and cut off from the rest of Germany. For the Kriegsmarine, keeping these isolated forces supplied with food, ammunition and everything else they needed to hold out against the strong Soviet attack became an increasing priority, despite the shortage of oil and particularly coal for the ships. In order to balance the competing demands for the dwindling reserves of fuel, Dönitz was given sole control of the transport and supply of coal, but his task was made almost impossible by the damage to the transport networks done by Allied air raids.

One other problem was minelaying by the RAF in the western and central Baltic, which caused the heaviest losses for German shipping, and also delayed ships' return trips, as cleared passages were almost immediately mined again. Therefore at this stage Dönitz had to prioritise military traffic, such as the withdrawal of forces from Norway and Denmark to bolster threatened fronts and the evacuation of the wounded from Kurland, rather than the evacuation of the rising numbers of civilian refugees. Later on, however, this would become of increasing importance. Dönitz was also faced with problems in the other areas of the naval war, like the North Sea and Norway, and the bases still holding out in France, Italy and on the islands of the Aegean.

Because of these problems, the resumption of the U-boat war with the new Type XXI and XXIII submarines, which until January 1945 had the first place in Dönitz's efforts, was more and more delayed by difficulties in training, but more so by the effects of the Allied air attacks against the building yards, which prevented the many newly commissioned boats being made ready for sea. So only one Type XXIII boat began its first war patrol at the end of January, followed until May by only five more, and a solitary Type XXI boat finally left on patrol on 30 April. So all the other problems became more important for Dönitz's daily work and he had to accept the failure of his hopes.

As Lüdde-Neurath was a direct witness to all the events and decisions, his 'diary' allows the reader to understand the problems of the time for Dönitz as commander-in-chief of the navy, and particularly when he succeeded Hitler as head of state, much better than other publications.

Jürgen Rohwer
2010

Section I

The Dönitz Government –
The Last Days of the Third Reich

Walter Lüdde-Neurath

Author's Foreword, 1948

In September 1944 I was appointed Adjutant to the Commander-in-Chief Kriegsmarine, which involved my being withdrawn from the fighting front against my wishes. When reporting to my new chief, Grossadmiral Dönitz, I made this clear to him. He rightly put me in my place, but in the succeeding months I continued to express my feelings on the matter freely. In captivity I maintained the same frankness. The chairman of the British denazification review board, which in 1947 decided into what category of 'militarist' I fell, took the view after a one-hour hearing that I had 'at least made an honest impression', which the board was benevolent enough to take into account. In my narrative hereunder I have attempted to remain faithful to this principle.

I am not presuming to write 'history'. I therefore relate my experiences in the first person and have not employed the abstract way of presenting events. The foundation for my account is the contemporaneous record I kept setting out the occurrences, decisions and conversations in which Grossadmiral Dönitz was involved during the period of the collapse. I have enhanced these notes with observations I made in my capacity as adjutant to the last, short-lived head of state of the Third Reich. Additionally I have available to me reports by other participants at the time, and the published literature regarding the collapse which has become available in the meantime.

A critical appraisal of this historical epoch and the current material being published requires a comprehensive study of the sources and literature, which is the preserve of the historian. I am not one. It is my purpose to throw light on the last phase of the Second World War in Europe from my own standpoint. It was a narrow view, increasingly reduced to an ever-smaller geographical area, which concluded with the supreme leadership being cut off not only from the outside world, but also from the greater part of Germany.

In order not to give a false picture I have avoided inserting knowledge gained later in the guise of contemporary opinions. I have only given house-room to my own deductions and conclusions where they appear necessary for a better understanding of matters under consideration or their significance for the present.

Accordingly it is my aim to provide the reader with an account that is as accurate as possible, and the researcher with an account from the tense and portentous situation of those days for historically objective consideration.

W. Lüdde-Neurath
Spring, 1948

Author's Foreword to the Second Edition, 1953

The acceptance of my work by the public, and the recognition afforded it by the experts give me cause to render special thanks to the Musterschmidt editorial house and the Institut für Völkerrecht (Institute for International Law) at the University of Göttingen as publisher.

At this time not all archives have been returned to the competent German authorities. Accordingly it has not been possible to resolve all the conflicting interpretations arising from the various texts and instruments of surrender signed at Rheims and Berlin in 1945. Meanwhile, a series of English-language publications has shed light on the dramatic events of the capitulation from the Allied viewpoint. According to these, it was intended to have the German government sign a treaty under German constitutional law. The document, worked out by the victors at long conferences and ready for signature, was scrapped at the last moment after the German negotiators had arrived at Rheims. SHAEF in Europe replaced it with a purely military instrument, aware now that the Germans would not sign any such treaty, which would ensure an unnecessary continuation of the fighting if a remedy was not found.

Deflected from their original intentions, Allied politicians had a major dilemma which they solved by overthrowing the Third Reich Caretaker Government and offering in place of the missing treaty a unilateral declaration that the capitulation of 'Germany' had 'gone through'.

A study of Allied sources confirms the German point of view: *The signed instruments of capitulation are purely military in character. They contain nothing authorising the victors to usurp the function of the German Government and carve up Germany amongst themselves. In the absence of a treaty to that effect signed by the German Government, in law the 1945 catastrophe did not deprive the German people of the right to the continuity and unity of the Reich.*

Walter Lüdde-Neurath
Spring 1953

Publisher's Foreword to the Third Edition, 1964

That the 'Dönitz Government' has not been considered adequately with due urgency by researchers in German Constitutional and International Law may result from the chaotic situation which prevailed during the collapse of Germany in 1945, and the inability or reluctance of the survivors, dedicated to rebuilding work, to address the spectre of our country's past death agonies.

Did the Dönitz Government, this remnant of German sovereign power in total collapse, have solely an historical function to wind-up the defunct Nazi regime, or should it have had a role in the founding of the new post-war state? This question for academic historians runs parallel to the questions of legality and legitimacy, the structure and form the new government should have had, what national and international recognition it ought to have expected and its position in the process of maintaining Germany's continuity and sovereignty.

Recognising the need to assemble and preserve the historical material related to this problem, my predecessor Professor Herbert Kraus, as Director of the Institute for International Law at Göttingen University, published this memoir of the personal adjutant to Grossadmiral Dönitz in two editions in 1950 and 1953. In this third edition the author, publishing house and I all considered the question whether the literature that has appeared in the intervening decade should also be taken into consideration. We were agreed that it would be a mistake to deprive the text of its originality as a personal memoir, which is primary material in conjunction with the accompanying documentation. The memoir has therefore only been augmented by some recently available documents, and by minor corrections here and there. On the other hand it did seem necessary to provide an Appendix describing the state of modern academic research into the 'Dönitz Government' written by an expert historian specialising in the era of the collapse.

From the abundant memoirs and significantly smaller stock of academic material and writings, Professor Walter Baum has assembled a collage of events assessing the reasons for the appointment of Dönitz as successor to Hitler, his plenipotentiary powers and his aims, the establishment of the 'Caretaker Reich Government', the circumstances surrounding the capitulation and what the word implied, and finally the arrest of the ministers and disbandment of the Flensburg enclave.

It is our hope that the combination of the author's conscientious memoir and the urgency of the academic investigation in combination will lead to the clarification of a portentous episode in our most recent history for both the historian and the lawyer.

Professor Georg Erler
Director, Institut für Völkerrecht, Göttingen University
Spring 1964

Chapter 1

Autumn 1944 to April 1945: Impressions at Führer-Headquarters

On 1 September 1944 I reported to Grossadmiral Dönitz, Commander-in-Chief of the Kriegsmarine, as his new adjutant. I was not known to him, and for my part I had only seen him fleetingly twice during military reviews.

In my career I had never had anything to do with High Command staffs and had never wished to. I would rather have remained at sea. I had just taken command of a fine torpedo boat and I shuddered at the thought of being shorebound as an adjutant. Thus I was anything but delighted by this new post. Upon introducing myself Dönitz took the wind out of my sails with a few choice words. Then he went on: 'I don't want courtiers and lackeys around me. I don't want to hear the echo of my own opinions coming from you, but only what you think personally. You can and should give me your honest beliefs, even if you are certain that the competent authorities or I think differently. That is the reason why I have brought an officer from the fighting front to fill this position. Should I become aware that you are repeating my ideas, or the words you speak have some ulterior motive behind them – you are out on your ear!' With that I was dismissed so that my predecessor could instruct me in my duties.

Fourteen days later I accompanied Dönitz for the first time to Führer Headquarters (FHQ). At the time it went under the codename *Wolfsschanze** and was located between the East Prussian lakes near the small town of Rastenburg close to the Görlitz forestry house. The large well-camouflaged

---

* Wolf's Lair.

installation was partitioned into three concentric restricted areas fenced off from each other. Each could only be entered with the corresponding special pass. The innermost restricted area contained only the Führer-bunker – a concrete cube of middle height– and the situation bunker. Access was permitted only to Hitler's personal staff, his SS bodyguard, an SD[†] detachment and his indispensable assistants. Everybody else, even those who had served at HQ for years, were barred. An officer who had spent more than six months in the immediate vicinity, in the Wehrmacht Command Staff barracks hut, told me that he had never seen Hitler face to face.

Whoever went into the innermost area for the first time had to submit beforehand to a body search carried out by the SD. I was informed that one must enter the holy of holies unarmed and that the security detail had the job of ensuring that this standing order was rigidly enforced. Naturally this did not go down too well with us weapons-bearers of the Reich, but I could understand the reasoning of the regime, given the events of 20 July past.

In mid-September 1944 Hitler, who until then by a massive effort of will had managed to hide any effects of the assassination attempt, suffered a relapse due to shock. He rarely left his bunker and even the military situation conferences were held only once a day, in his private room in the presence of the smallest possible group necessary for it. Accordingly several days passed before I was admitted to deliver my report as ordered.

I was disappointed by Hitler's outward appearance. He was shorter than I had pictured him, walked with a stoop and – contrary to the photos which the censors let through – seemed fumbling and unceremonious. Nevertheless I was not able to shake myself free of a certain suggestive effect. From my first impressions and later observations, this seemed to emanate predominantly from his gaze and voice. Besides Hitler I was introduced to other leading personalities of the Third Reich. Thus in the first few days I had personal audiences with Göring and Himmler, Keitel and Jodl, Bormann and numerous others who either belonged to Hitler's permanent entourage or with whom I came into contact at military situation conferences at FHQ. My first

---

[†] *Sicherheitdienst* – the Nazi Party's intelligence and security body.

impressions here were naturally too fleeting to deserve retention, and in several cases I had to revise them later. As a curiosity I might just mention in passing that in the entourage of the 'Führer and Reich Chancellor' I scarcely ever saw a civilian dressed as one. Even as a professional military man I found it impossible to correctly identify the diversity of non-military uniforms and rank insignia. Even the purely civilian stenographers wore military-type livery. On my first visit to FHQ it was not intended merely that I should make character studies but rather that I should brief myself on the military situation and the basis for those hopes by which the multitudes of fighting men and the people in general were encouraged to stick to their guns. In this respect I formed the following picture. The morale of those around Hitler was admittedly low but not despairing. The acute dangers which had threatened the survival of the Reich, the serious setbacks in the summer of 1944 – the successful Allied landings in the West, the collapse of Army Group Centre in the East, the assassination attempt of 20 July – seemed to have been warded off. There was new hope, basically propped up on three legs:

(1) Contrary to the predictions of most senior military commanders, the enemy in the West had been halted before he reached the Reich frontier and was now opposed by a cohesive and strengthening front. Holding the Maginot Line and the Westwall with the Rhine to the rear, no immediate danger was perceived at present.

(2) As a result of the failed assassination plot of 20 July, the regime felt strengthened in its position and in its self-confidence. It was believed that not only the conspirators who were actively involved in the 'treason' had been unmasked, but that wider circles which were considered 'guilty' on account of passive resistance or had become resigned to the 'sabotage of total war' had been taken out of the reckoning. By the 'cleansing measures' and transfer of the Replacements-Training Army (*Ersatzheer*) to Himmler, which had resulted in harsh discipline to reorganise the Western Front, the Army High Command could now promise a stiffening of the inner will to resist and through that the outer strength to do so.

(3) The principal reason for optimism was the expectation of a swift end to the bombing terror. This was based on current fighter production and the

planned introduction of the Me 262 jet fighter. Armaments production was running flat out, its main output being panzers, infantry weapons, fighter aircraft, V-weapons and U-boats. The assembly lines were located for the most part in underground factories out of the reach of enemy bomber formations. The highest production statistics were achieved during the period of the heaviest terror-bombing: in July 1944 almost 4,000 fighters came off the assembly lines while the highest monthly quota of U-boats delivered, thirty-seven boats, was achieved in December 1944. Fighter aircraft production was maintained in the subsequent period to the year's end at a monthly average of 2,000 units.[1]

From these figures it can be understood how Karl Saur, head of the Production Office at the Armaments Ministry, was able to tell me with complete confidence when I introduced myself to him in September 1944 that: 'By Christmas we shall have air supremacy!' (At that time I was unaware that Saur tended to be extremely optimistic about the numbers of units coming off the production lines and the time required for them to become operational.)

The military leadership considered that air supremacy over the Reich was a precondition for a change in Germany's fortunes. The next stage was explained to me by Dönitz (I never heard Hitler speak on the subject) in roughly the following terms: 'Once we have the roof over Germany the fronts will hold. Then we can start hitting back with the long-range V-weapons and the new U-boats to make Britain not only ready for peace but perhaps anxious for it. Sooner or later the moment of realisation will come for the British, who think like shopkeepers, that the sacrifice in blood and financial investment is not worth the candle. Then we shall have created a basis on which Germany can negotiate and be spared unconditional surrender.'

There is no doubt that the later course of events showed this line of thinking to be absurd. In the autumn of 1944, however, even I clung to this pale shaft of light, especially in the U-boat building sector where I had special knowledge, and upon which our hopes had a real basis.[2] But the premise for the end of 1944, the 'roof over Germany', was illusory. How illusory would soon be proved.

At the beginning of December, Adolf Hitler, after a brief sojourn at the Reich Chancellery, moved into his FHQ *Adlerhorst*[‡] near Bad Nauheim. It was situated on a wooded slope and consisted of a few bunkers. Since it had insufficient space for the permanent staff and visitors, they were accommodated either in surrounding facilities or in special trains parked outside tunnels, into which they would be shunted should the air-raid alarm sound. The Western Front was once more a priority for the main effort.

Early on 16 December the Wehrmacht embarked upon its last great attack, the Ardennes Offensive. The strategic aim was to recapture Antwerp, thus dividing the British and US forces, and encircling Montgomery's Army Group. Thirty-two divisions and 1,400 panzers – the greatest number ever assembled by Germany at any time in the war for an offensive – were made ready in great secrecy. The enemy was taken completely by surprise. Weather unsuitable for flying prevailed, deep penetration was achieved at the first attempt, and territory quickly won. After a few days when the aircraft of both sides were operational again the thrust petered out: in essence as a result of the oppressive enemy aerial superiority, whose machines not only participated successfully in the ground fighting, but also cut off supplies to the very narrow spearheads, these being forced to use the roads because of the nature of the terrain.

More bitter than the disappointment at this failure was the knowledge obtained at the same time that the dream of air supremacy over the Reich was a mere flight of fancy. The newly equipped Luftwaffe fighter arm consisted predominantly of the 'tried and tested' Me 109 and Fw 190. Doubts, often loudly expressed, as to whether these were a match for modern enemy fighters, were met with: 'The type is equal, the greater number will be decisive.' The greater number was nothing of the kind. There was a slight superiority in type, but the important factor was the battle experience of the enemy 'old hands' who had felt at home over Germany for the past year, and who were faced by young, poorly trained German pilots who, lacking combat experience and often adequate flying hours, were thrown into the fray at the

---

[‡] Eagle Eyrie.

deep end. The ratio of victories rose to 10:1 against, and eventually on cloudless days it was thought prudent that Luftwaffe fighters of these types should be grounded to save fuel and lives.

Great efforts were now made to get the jet fighters operational. As combat results showed, they were the type we needed. Despite all difficulties production was satisfactory. Yet from the completion of the individual aircraft to its operational readiness at a trained combat unit there was a long wearisome path requiring time, space and fuel even under normal circumstances. The courser of events in the spring of 1945 definitively overwhelmed these preconditions. The jet-fighter arm never made it.[3]

On 12 January 1945 the Soviets began their winter offensive along the entire Eastern Front. They opened a decisive breach at Baranov on the Vistula bridgehead which collapsed the German front.[4] In a fast and virtually unhindered advance, the Russian spearheads penetrated deeply into the Upper Silesian industrial region and reached the Oder at Küstrin and Frankfurt. The East Prussian 'fortress' shrank in size daily. The long and lightly defended front between Danzig and Küstrin protected the province of Pomerania, as yet untouched by the enemy. At the end of January 1945, a surprise German thrust eastwards from there attempted to relieve the threat to Berlin but failed almost before it had began. In the view of the Reich Chancellery (Hitler's HQ from mid-January 1945 until his death), this was due to defeatism amongst the troops and their commanders. Zhukov now swept through Pomerania and readied himself behind the Oder at leisure for the final blow.

In the West after the failure of the Ardennes Offensive, German troops retired in stages across the Rhine. According to a report by the then US Chief of the General Staff General Marshall, this last bulwark was overcome surprisingly quickly by the capture intact of the bridge over the Rhine at Remagen on 7 March.

Despite this hopeless situation the man in the bunker at the Reich Chancellery, obsessed by the idea of a controlling Providence, did not give up. It is possible that his belief in his 'mission', in which he identified every new blow of fate only as a harsher test of his mettle, was decisive, although objective considerations did play a role and were at least discussed within his immediate circle. Dönitz and Jodl were agreed that the war should be continued in spite of their realising the inevitability of military defeat. This arose not only from military obedience but also inner conviction.

Behind the decision to hold out at all costs was the enemy demand for 'unconditional surrender'. Since the Casablanca Conference of January 1943, this was the spectre which throttled all German peace initiatives at birth and was the best foundation possible for 'total war'. Hitler particularly allowed himself no illusions regarding the grave consequences for the entire German people of an unconditional military capitulation. Now and again he would describe these consequences in the most harrowing terms. The agreement at Yalta regarding the envisaged carving-up and dismemberment of Germany was known. FHQ had a captured map from the British 'Operation Eclipse' in which the frontier between West and East was etched in that same prominent manner which would later become bitter reality as the Iron Curtain. The effects of the predicted occupation, division and strangulation of the nation were painted very darkly with regard to the biological stock, in which a reduction of the population by twenty to thirty million within a generation was foreseen. Here was the reason why no stone had to be left unturned in the effort to avert such a catastrophe. History would not condemn the casualty lists, but only ask if everything had been done to prevent the outcome. Moreover, there was an obligation to the population of the Eastern provinces, if the Soviet advance could not be held, to evacuate the people to the West. It may be debated whether this task justified the prolongation of the already-lost war. What is in any case certain is that to have abandoned the refugees and soldiers in the East to the mercy of the Russians at the capitulation would have been criminal. The impatient populace of Western Germany considered that every day the war went on was criminal madness, while millions in the East hoped for its continuation for as long as it took for them to escape the bestial horrors of a Russian occupation. How the differing outlooks of the East and West German populations influenced the course of the final phase of the war, and effectively delayed its termination, is examined more closely in later chapters.

Yet another argument for the continuation of the war in the spring of 1945 was the fear of surrendering during the winter which had to avoided at all costs in the interests of the troops, since experience had shown that complications arose when the enemy took over logistics. Jodl expounded this point of view at Nuremberg, having been proved at least partially right by the events in the prisoner-of-war camps of all victorious powers after the capitulation, even though it came at the beginning of the summer.

Finally it was undoubtedly the hope for a change in the political situation, a split between the Allies, which significantly strengthened the will of the German leaders to hold out. This hope was fuelled from various sources. First, and probably most importantly, they wanted to believe it. Secondly, from the conviction that in Britain the time would soon come when it was realised they were 'slaughtering the wrong pig' and that Britain would also be a loser if Germany went down in total defeat. The war had begun to liberate Poland, and to disable Germany, which had become too strong a power on the European continent. Instead, there had been a total turnaround, providing the spectre of a Soviet Union with a much stronger economic and human potential at the door, while Poland had not been saved but engulfed. Dönitz put it thus: 'Churchill will perhaps go down in history as a victor in the Second World War, but at the same time as the man who dug the grave for the British Empire.' From the RSHA Abwehr daily bulletins every enemy report which mentioned tensions on the Allied front or signs of a possible rupture in their relationship was taken out and highlighted. The German leadership therefore did not dismiss the possibility of political change nor some other 'miracle'.[5] Such a change, however, could only be of use if Germany was still 'alive'. One does not commit suicide voluntarily now (unconditional surrender) just because death is bound to come eventually in the future. So, hold out! And for as long as humanly possible, for the closer the fronts of West and East approached each other, the more likely was the breach in this coalition formed only for the negative purpose of destroying Germany. When that moment came, one had to be standing. So, fight on!

In mid-March the objective was to hold the Oder front and hurl back the enemy across the Rhine. For this purpose, 12.Armee was formed under General Wenck in the Harz. The last hopes rested upon it. Arms and equipment were apparently still available. For the most part these troops were officer-aspirants and military cadets, and represented an elite for the time, but they were never employed for their the original task of liberating the Reich in the West and driving the Anglo-Americans back across the Rhine.

At the beginning of April the increasing disintegration of the Western Front and the imminent major offensive in the East led to predictions that the Allied armies would meet in central Germany. For this eventuality, Hitler gave Generalfeldmarschall Kesselring South Germany, and Grossadmiral Dönitz North Germany, to continue the defence. No executive powers accompanied this provisional arrangement which would only come into effect upon receipt of a special order and only in the region where Hitler was not present. In which direction he would head was left open. His inclinations, the military circumstances and the actual preparations being made by his personal followers led one to believe that for a long defence he would decide in favour of the more suitable if less well-equipped southern sector.

On 16 April 1945 with their major offensive on the Oder front, the Russians opened the last chapter of the great military struggle. The Germans fought a bitter defensive battle, the infantry shoulder to shoulder with the Volkssturm, men from the Kriegsmarine and Luftwaffe, and police in a desperate fight not to yield an inch of territory. Anti-aircraft guns had been transferred from all corners of the Reich to help bombard the Russian positions. The front held for three days before the physical and material possibility of resistance began to falter. The batteries were left without ammunition, the last drop of fuel was consumed. No resupply was possible because the transport system had been demolished and the enemy had total air supremacy. On the afternoon of 19 April 1945 the enemy crossed the Oder via the bridgeheads south of Wriezen and east of Müncheberg, and crushed the last vestiges of an intact German front underfoot.

From 22 April Dönitz and I watched the Battle for Berlin as spectators from afar as it hastened towards its culmination. Next day we learned of Hitler's decision to remain in the capital. His main reasoning here must have been that if the capital of the Reich fell, the war would be lost irrevocably, although he would of course never discount the vague hope of some miracle flowing from his deranged belief in 'Providence' to save the day at the last moment. On the other hand, he voiced his belief that a successful relief of Berlin would bring about a reversal of the military tide together with the psychological one, something like 'the liberation of Stalingrad for the Russians'. Hitler still believed in the power of his personality to motivate. His remaining in the encircled capital would encourage his forces to do their uttermost. He was going to lead the defence personally and – through the OKW which he had sent to the North for the purpose – the relief of Berlin as well. On paper there actually were sufficient numbers to imagine success on the fronts around Berlin: Armee Busse made up from Schörner's fragmented Armee in the South-east: III.Panzerkorps under Steiner from the north and Armee Wenck from the west would attempt to break the Russian encirclement. For a short time it would be possible to restore contact with the defenders of Potsdam from the west. But the lack of supplies and mobility, the impossibility of establishing strongpoints and exploiting local successes, together with enemy air supremacy, brought all efforts, and all personal bravery, of which even now there were countless instances, to nothing.

The hopelessness of the struggle was made clear by Jodl in his situation report delivered at Rheinsberg on 27 April. This OKW conference was attended by Keitel, Dönitz and Himmler. On 29 April the situation of Berlin became totally hopeless. On 30 April Hitler drew the necessary conclusion and at 1530 hrs ended his life with a bullet. He bequeathed the political legacy to the Commander-in-Chief of the Kriegsmarine, Grossadmiral Karl Dönitz.

Chapter 2

Dönitz Leaves Berlin

From the summer of 1943, the HQ of the Commander-in-Chief, Kriegsmarine and SKL§ had been at Bernau north of Berlin. Its proximity to the Reich capital, an excellent signals network, two rarely-used command bunkers and not least the quiet atmosphere of a country barracks, codenamed *Koralle* and hidden on the edge of a wood, made it an ideal command centre. When the Russians reached the central section of the Oder river and threatened Berlin. Dönitz reduced the Naval High Command rigorously and transferred it to North Germany to avoid exposing the entire command apparatus to the risk of surprise attack.

He personally decided to stay near Berlin with a small staff since he did not want to lose contact with the leaders of the state and Wehrmacht at this critical time. A special train, 'Auerhahn', was provided in the north-west of Berlin, well-camouflaged and ready to steam away at a moment's notice. The changeover did not go well, however, and while *Koralle* was being abandoned, I accompanied Dönitz to the daily situation conference at the Reich Chancellery, and from there back to the train. I do not have fond memories of my arrival at this new command centre and of my first hours there. The detaching of a number of coaches for the SKL, the loss of power and signals facilities during all the shunting, the generally cramped conditions, the blackout and air-raid alarms put the 'Lion' – a nickname he had earned with the U-boat arm – into very bad sorts. I was prompted to suggest very quickly that he should return to *Koralle* with his personal staff and await future developments in peace, and not transfer out until the Army General Staff gave

---

§ *Seekriegsleitung* – Naval Intelligence.

warning of imminent danger of a Soviet breakthrough. He accepted this idea and it proved satisfactory.

Dönitz attended the situation conferences at FHQ two or three times weekly. Through his personal advisor, Konteradmiral Wagner, supported by a specialist aide in surface and U-boat operations, he held the reins of the Kriegsmarine in his hands. This way of doing things was − from the personal and tactical point of view − a really favourable solution given the circumstances, but the constant rising and falling rumble of artillery on the distant front line was such that the question plagued us constantly − how much longer do we have?

On the morning of 16 April an enormous increase in the sounds of battle announced the beginning of the Russian spring offensive before we even learned of it by wire or radio. Dönitz put his staff at one hour's readiness, which meant that upon receipt of the order we had to be ready to decamp within an hour. We now attended the situation conference at the Reich Chancellery bunker daily. Hopes rose when 18 April came and went and the enemy had not broken through. I heard Keitel recall the 'old saying from experience' that an attack bogged down if it did not achieve a breakthrough by the third day. Despite this and other platitudes, the evening of 19 April found Dönitz seized by a strange disquiet. Shortly after I bade him goodnight he rang me: 'I don't like it. We shall move out at 2330 hrs.' I glanced at the time: we had barely an hour. In great haste but in good order we vacated our quarters in accordance with the previously prepared plan and at 2330 hrs on the dot − only a few hours before the arrival of the Russians − our small convoy of cars moved off into the night to the thunder of the guns, a roar of motors, small-arms fire, bursting artillery shells and a sky swept by searchlights.

Our destination was Berlin-Dahlem, which we reached just after midnight on 20 April. Here at Dönitz's instructions I arranged his service quarters into an auxiliary command post. The staff was housed in the actual building, the signals troop in an annexe. A motorised radio unit, some telephone and telex connections and a small private bunker, the long passages of which were already occupied by people from the neighbouring houses, completed the picture of this very makeshift Kriegsmarine HQ.

On the early afternoon of 20 April, Hitler's birthday, I accompanied Dönitz once more to the Reich Chancellery. I saw the Führer close-to for the last time. I was just entering the bunker as Hitler left his private quarters, and fell in on the left wing of a rather short queue waiting to congratulate him. When delivering our situation report at the conference afterwards, I had the opportunity to study him freely. His speech and eyes were as expressive as always. His mental powers seemed intact. He was by no means a 'lunatic' in the normally understood sense, but physically he was a beaten and broken man; bloated, bent, feeble and nervous.

On this day Hitler gave effect to his order for the defence of the North region, by which Dönitz received territorial jurisdiction but no operational power of command. He could give instructions to civilian offices but not to forces on the military land fronts apart from the Kriegsmarine (Appendix 2). On the afternoon of 21 April, Dönitz and Hitler met for the last time. The city centre was already being shelled by the Soviets from the northern out-skirts. In view of the immediate threat of encirclement, Dönitz was released to take up his appointment. I had been detached from the entourage before-hand to prepare for the move northwards. After careful consideration of the air raid situation, it was decided that 0200 hrs on 22 April was most favourable time to move. The last preparations were made with the air-raid sirens howling.

When we set out it was still relatively quiet. Our convoy negotiated the last gap in the encirclement to the north-west of the capital, but made slow progress. Checkpoints, obstructions, and street barricades laid out in nearly every village reduced our speed to a crawl. Frequently we took cover during fighter-bomber alarms, but our convoy was never attacked directly. Allied pilots had better targets nearby, and for this purpose tended to follow the high-ways, which we avoided for that reason. This brought us into contact with streams of refugees and Wehrmacht columns in retreat. These were thicker on the ground the further north we drove. Whereas the refugees, despite their misery, still managed to give an impression of being under some kind of orderly leadership, we found the signs of disintegration amongst the staffs and fighting men extremely depressing. Etched into the features of each was the cause of this great emigration – fear.

On the late afternoon of 22 April we arrived at our new HQ at Plön/ Holstein. A couple of barrack huts on a lakeside had been made available to Dönitz and his staff. Thanks to the well-versed signals unit – they had already been here for some weeks – we had adequate wireless and radio communications to all command centres in the northern region and the still-intact foreign posts. Our signals platoon even managed to obtain secure links with Berlin and the southern region for us.

It was from here at Plön that within a few days Dönitz would emerge from his very restricted sphere of operations to lead the Reich, and I too would experience the final days of the Second World War and the Third Reich at the very heart of events. Those in positions of responsibility who led Germany in the short but eventful period which was to follow were condemned to silence, some for long years, others permanently. All files, documents and even personal notes were confiscated and remained inaccessible to German researchers for an indefinite period. At the time of writing in 1964, publications to date concerning this important historical period are therefore limited officially to such selected biased and partial material as the victors care to reveal, and unofficially we have personal memoirs, narratives, assumptions and a nice line in lies and distortions. I therefore consider it to be my duty, being someone whose knowledge of this short period of German history, in which I was not a principal actor but heard and remembered what transpired, to preserve and lay bare the facts of what actually occurred in the days when the Third Reich died. This is as good a place as any to render an account of my insight into events, which forms the basis for this book. I leave researchers and readers to draw their own conclusions as to the completeness and honesty of the presentation.

From taking up the post of Adjutant to the Kriegsmarine Commander-in-Chief in September 1944 until our move on 19 April 1945, I performed the usual duties of an ADC. I administered personnel, was at Dönitz's side constantly, and took part in all his military conferences within the Kriegsmarine, although not at conferences attended by those of equal or higher rank than he. My appreciation of the great happenings up to the collapse of the Eastern Front is therefore based on occasional attendances at Hitler's situation conferences, the daily written resumé of the same, on experiences and conversations of an unofficial nature in the Reich Chancellery, and on many talks with Dönitz frequently in private and on a basis of trust. Since at first he directed his dealings and ideas exclusively towards his own sphere of operations and showed no interest in any other portfolio, I have intentionally kept my account of events up to April 1945 brief in the expectation that more competent writers than I are available to examine this period.

With our transfer to the northern region, Dönitz became its First Man. Later he became so in all Germany by his appointment as Hitler's successor over all those who until then had been outside his authority and jurisdiction (e.g, Keitel and Himmler). It will accordingly be clear at this stage that with very few exceptions I took part personally at all conferences. I had noticed how Hitler had a record made by uniformed stenographers of every word spoken. There was no such arrangement for Dönitz's staff, and so I began to take brief notes of the events and main points, and with Dönitz's agreement from 2 May 1945 began to keep 'The Grossadmiral's War Diary' which I would type directly into the machine from my notes. Both sets of these 'daily minutes' were confiscated when we were taken prisoner, but I managed to hold on to the notes. The last time I had them in my hand was at the end of September 1945 in my cell at Nuremberg Prison, when I was allowed to remove a few utensils from my baggage. Six weeks later I was transferred to the 'witnesses' wing' of the same prison. Here I was informed officially by a US sergeant that documents and similar material which we had had as prisoners and which might be of evidentiary value at the Nuremberg Trials should be returned to their owners. I thought that Dönitz's defence attorneys would find my diary useful and asked for it. Unfortunately it 'could no longer be found' and all my complaints and the attempts by the defence to discover its whereabouts were unsuccessful.

By then I had already begun to write my memoir. The events were still fresh in my mind. During the two years or so I spent in captivity, I had had plenty of time and opportunity to discuss events with other participants. Finally I saved a series of notes, some of which Dönitz had dictated to me immediately after our arrest, and some of which had been made available to me during the trial. They left the internment camp in the plaster cast on the arm of an 'unlucky' comrade. Some time later I followed equally illegally (if by another route) and had the good luck to obtain a copy of the 'daily min-utes' from a senior US military centre while posing under an assumed name.[1] Therefore I think I can guarantee the accuracy of the facts and motives set out in the succeeding chapters. For a better understanding I have arranged the occurrences, unfolding with increasing rapidity and intensity, by theme rather than in a purely chronological sequence, which appears instead in a 'timetable' alongside the Introduction to this book.

Chapter 3

An Impossible Job – Defend the Northern Region

In the late autumn of 1944 Dönitz still considered his main task as Kriegsmarine Commander-in-Chief to be the building-up of the U-boat arm. He never allowed the leadership of the 'Fourth Arm of the Wehrmacht', as it was referred to half-jokingly, half-maliciously within the Kriegsmarine, to be delegated to anyone else during throughout the war. The U-boat arm was technically, tactically and organisationally his own work. The U-boat arm and Dönitz had grown great together.

At the outbreak of war Germany had only a small number of operational U-boats, substantially below the limit agreed under the London Naval Treaty of 1935. Not until September 1939, after the declaration of war, was U-boat construction and crew training begun in earnest, and by 1942 they were causing Britain great concern. The improvement in aerial radar coverage over the whole North Atlantic introduced by Britain in May 1943 checkmated this most powerful German weapon at a stroke. Its decisive significance was emphasised by Churchill throughout the war. Overnight the entire carefully-built U-boat fleet was rendered next to useless. Successes sank to a minimum, and losses soared. In the summer of 1943 every second or third boat was sunk in action, and a newly commissioned boat had little prospect of surviving more than two patrols. That despite this catastrophic adverse ratio between losses and successes the morale and will to fight of the U-boat crews remained at the same outstanding level to the last day of the war speaks volumes for the value of Dönitz's leadership, this being where his main strength lay.

After the collapse of the U-boat War, Dönitz devoted all his energies to the creation of new U-boat types. The problem was quickly solved. From the previous 'submersible', the true 'undersea-boat' followed which could spend long periods submerged and, as was proven, escape completely from the clutches of radar and air reconnaissance. High underwater speed and modern detection equipment gave the new types excellent prospects for success against convoy traffic and escorts. From the end of 1944 this new kind of boat began to leave the yards in increasing numbers, but its operational use was frustrated by events in the spring of 1945. That the U-boat arm was no longer decisive was probably clear to Dönitz by the time the Russians launched their January offensive, when the priorities of the Kriegsmarine underwent a decisive shift.

The large-scale repatriation of German troops began following the defection of Finland from the Axis in the summer of 1944. The transports continued with the collapse of the two Baltic fronts and the return of military units from Norway, and reached their high point in the spring of 1945 with the evacuation of the German populations of East and West Prussia and finally Pomerania. In an unceasing operation, all Kriegsmarine and mercantile vessels capable of sailing were diverted into this German equivalent of 'Dunkirk'. According to reports of the time, about two million Germans were saved from the Bolshevists. The job was at the forefront of Dönitz's priorities in the closing months of the war and seemed to him more important than the idea of an immediate capitulation. He therefore welcomed Hitler's decision to give him control over the distribution of coal and fuel oil in the northern region at the beginning of April, thus enabling him to better regulate the evacuation transports.

Hitler's order dividing the Reich into North (Dönitz) and South (Kesselring) followed on 15 April. This edict was only provisional and, since it bestowed no executive power on the holders, was treated as merely informative and as an organisational guide for us when making preparations. From 22 April, when the capital was almost completely surrounded, and our separation from Berlin had become inevitable, Dönitz put these preparations into effect at his new Plön HQ. On 20 April he had received nominal power of command over the territory of the northern region including the civilian sector (Appendix 2), but the authority to wield the power of command still did not come into effect because Hitler (in Berlin) intended to retain power through the OKW at Rheinsberg until his reign ended.

For me there is no doubt that Dönitz initially proposed to defend the northern region to the best of his ability if only through his conviction as to the need for the repatriation of military personnel and civilians alluded to earlier. His military self-discipline, loyalty to the Führer and no doubt his previous efforts also played a role in his will to create for the Reich, the German Navy and himself an honourable exit, which he considered to be endangered by backsliding, treachery and the chaos it threatened. Accordingly he discussed in earnest how best to defend Northern Germany with General Kinzel, head of Command Staff North, one of the staffs set up purposely for the northern region, and Gauleiter Wegener, who at Dönitz's suggestion had been nominated by Hitler as the supreme civilian Reich Defence Commissioner for Northern Germany. They realised that a long defence was impossible. In the areas under discussion (Mecklenburg, Schleswig-Holstein and northern Lower Saxony) weapons supply from the manufacturers was no longer possible. Heavy weapons and *Panzerfäuste* were not produced in the region at all. It would therefore be necessary to make do with what was available. The same went for the supply of oil and coal. How catastrophic the situation had become here can best be seen from the serious attempts made to convert railway locomotives from coal to wood firing. Food was guaranteed only for so long as Mecklenburg held out, the major stocks, particularly of potatoes, being warehoused there. On the occasion of the OKW visit to Rheinsberg on 27 April, Dönitz held talks with Generalmajor von Trotha, Chief of the Army Group Vistula Staff, now located on the western side of the Oder. Von Trotha confirmed that contrary to what OKW might think, there was no prospect of holding Mecklenburg, and from the point of view of food supply no possibility of a protracted resistance existed.

The additional chapter on the overall military situation rounds off the picture. Total enemy occupation of the northern region would follow once the Western Allies made a determined effort to do so. A few days remained which Dönitz would attempt to extend in order to get the returning vessels home and keep the Baltic shuttle running for as long as possible. He also tried to motivate the organisation of a rapid and orderly retreat on land, where the situation was equally grave, and here he enjoyed a certain degree of success. He would not entertain the idea of premature individual actions which could prejudice the successful completion of the repatriation, security and order in the region, however. He was against the plan for an independent surrender of Hamburg which Gauleiter Kaufmann had worked out with the City Commandant. Dönitz had heard about it from the Commander-in-Chief, North West, Generalfeldmarschall Busch, and primarily from the head of the Inland SD, Ohlendorf, whose intelligence network was first class, and he read Kaufmann's appeal verbatim from the Hamburg wire broadcasting service even before Kaufmann had broadcast it. It appeared to Dönitz that his own aim – to keep Schleswig-Holstein free for the disembarkation of the shiploads of refugees from the East – might be seriously jeopardised by the loss of Hamburg. Kaufmann side-stepped attempts by Dönitz to meet him, and an exchange of phone calls and telegrams, though correct as always, was also unsuccessful. We received a telex at midday on 30 April, from which his intentions could be read between the lines. This happened just as Dönitz was about to leave for Lübeck to meet Himmler. They were of one accord on the Hamburg question and Dönitz ordered me to draft the reply. Himmler began to dictate his own reply off the cuff, and Dönitz attempted to deter him with the comment, 'Lüdde is already doing it'.

Since Himmler's outpouring was pathetic and impractical, Dönitz sent off my draft with his own signature appended. This document is reproduced at Appendix 4, since it shows clearly Dönitz's attitude and line of thought before he knew of Hitler's death and his own appointment as successor. When Dönitz received the nomination as head of state and Commander-in-Chief of the German forces in the North, because of Kaufmann's resolute stance and the rapidly developing general situation he decided to surrender Hamburg without a fight and ordered the troops out of the city. They left on 2 May, it not being practical to surrender the city before then on account of the start of negotiations with Montgomery that same evening (Appendix 8).

Seen overall, the order to Dönitz to defend the northern region was an impossible task, and was never confirmed officially. When Dönitz assumed overall responsibility on 30 April, a protracted defence was ruled out by the circumstances, and to his way of thinking would not be of much use towards ending hostilities. Nevertheless, ordering him to 'defend the northern region' prepared him for the resolution of the greater problem.

Chapter 4

Regarding the Succession to Hitler

On 30 January 1943 Dönitz became Commander-in-Chief, Kriegsmarine. His predecessor, Grossadmiral Raeder, had opposed Hitler's order to decommission all heavy warships and had been dismissed. The reason for Hitler's decision was the failure of the large units to achieve any 'appreciable' success since the loss of the *Bismarck* in May 1941. The immediate cause of the crisis was the failure of an anti-convoy operation in the Arctic on 31 December 1942. At dawn that day it had seemed initially that, after many attempts, the German naval force had managed to disperse the ring of escorts and savage a Murmansk convoy. The premature signal sent by a young U-boat commander, 'The battle has reached its climax. I see only red', aroused false hopes in the HQ of the 'Blue Tsar', Admiral Karls, Commander-in-Chief, Naval Group North, Kiel. These naturally found their way promptly to FHQ and Hitler's ear. The latter waited in tense expectation to hear from the situation reports of the next few days that he had material for a *Sondermeldung*.** Instead the operation ended with a meagre account of skirmishing in which both sides lost one destroyer and had one heavy cruiser damaged.

Hitler chose Dönitz as Raeder's successor because he saw in him a typical representative of the U-boat arm, able to realise at once what was required by way of cooperation and understanding of his plans. This was a mistaken conclusion. Thus Dönitz provided Hitler with a plan to decommission the big ships as ordered, but was convinced after examining the matter that Hitler's

---

** A Wehrmacht special communiqué issued to the public announcing an important event, most frequently a military victory.

decision and his own assent to it were wrong. Accordingly he flew back to FHQ and asked Hitler to revise his decision. This caused the only serious confrontation between them, but Hitler gave in. From this point onwards, Hitler always treated Dönitz with courtesy and respect. He never shouted at him, and never addressed him in any manner but as 'Herr Grossadmiral'. It was rare that any reproach was made: if it happened, he was spoken to in a businesslike manner, and his replies were frank and decisive. On the other hand Dönitz made an effort to gain the confidence of the supreme warlord, which he saw as indispensable for the command of the service with which he had been entrusted. He won it by unreserved candour in all questions of his sphere of responsibility. No failure was brushed under the carpet: he confessed his own errors before suspicion, and from it distrust, arose. Concerns about future or foreseen setbacks were admitted long beforehand, as for example the danger that the U-boat campaign would fold in the spring of 1943, the fears for the *Tirpitz* in late 1944 and the predicted delays in bringing into operation the new types of U-boat proof against enemy detection.

Dönitz deliberately limited his involvement in Kriegsmarine affairs and took no interest in politics, the Army High Command or other offices, but would tolerate no outside interference in the Kriegsmarine. On the basis of mutual trust and respect with Hitler, Dönitz created a special position at FHQ for himself. The Kriegsmarine remained the only portfolio, or at least the only branch of the Wehrmacht, which retained its independence to the end, and in which no outsider dared meddle. Even the restriction on the Wehrmacht judicial system in favour of the People's Court ordered by Hitler in the autumn of 1944 was expressly not applicable to the Kriegsmarine, and in the matter of the National Socialist Leadership Officers, Dönitz instituted a regulation which deprived the Party of all influence.

Beyond the trust and respect he had for Dönitz, in the final year of the war Hitler's concern for the life of the Grossadmiral became increasingly evident. This was shown by a strict ban on flying, frequent enquiries during air raids whether the Grossadmiral was in the bunker yet ('Damn, now there's nothing else for it, I suppose we have to go down') and finally the ban on leaving Reich territory. As in all previous years, Dönitz wanted to spend Christmas 1944 with his men at the front. At Hitler's request he had to cancel his planned journey to Libau, and also the Norwegian voyage which was to replace it and settle for being with Kriegsmarine units at Cuxhaven, although even here he was overwhelmed with security precautions. Conclusions as to the eventual succession – if Hitler even thought of Dönitz in this connection so early on – could not be drawn, since Hitler never mentioned the subject and Dönitz never gave it a thought.

* * *

By express declaration of the Führer and Reichs Chancellor in his Reichstag speech at the beginning of the war (Appendix 1), Hermann Göring was the 'second man in the state' and Hitler's predestined successor. His star waned, however, with the defeat of the Luftwaffe. At FHQ in the autumn of 1944 the accession of Göring was not only considered unthinkable but also insupportable. I remember well the general merriment at a remark Hermann had apparently made before a situation conference in October 1944: 'Good heavens, if the July plot had succeeded, I would have had to deal with it.' This observation did the rounds as the joke of the day, and was repeated by SS-Gruppenführer Fegelein that evening at the only non-official meeting of Himmler and Dönitz to take place while I was his adjutant. Here again laughter rang out. Himmler, suddenly becoming serious, turned to Dönitz and said, 'One thing is probably certain, Herr Grossadmiral, the Reichsmarschall would never have succeeded him.' Dönitz made no reply, but I interpreted his silence as agreement. At the time I thought that the forthright nature of Himmler's remark must be based on some arrangement of Hitler's unknown to me – either positive, in favour of some other person, or merely negative, in the rejection of Göring. Today I consider it more likely that Himmler was expressing his own decision not to recognise Göring as the successor.

That Hitler himself had also dropped the idea of Göring's succession was generally inferred from the palpable coolness and reserve with which he treated him at this time. I found this confirmed in the opinion of one of the Führer's adjutants with whom I was discussing the question of the succession at the beginning of April 1945 in the Reich Chancellery bunker. He mentioned the possibility, the first time I had heard it spoken, of the nomination of Dönitz and added, 'Whoever gets it, it won't be the Reichsmarschall.' Hitler's order on who should take supreme command when Germany was split into two parts (Kesselring, South: Dönitz, North) made it clearer. Officially, however, Göring's eligibility to the throne of the Third Reich was not invalidated until 23 April. On the evening of that day – by then we were at Plön – Bormann rang us from the Reich Chancellery: 'Hermann has putsched in the South and ordered most of the Reich Government in the North to come to him at once. We had to use all resources to hand to prevent the Reich Government people flying out. The Führer has relieved Göring of his post and appointed Generaloberst Ritter von Greim as the successor to Göring as Commander-in-Chief of the Luftwaffe, and promoted him Feldmarschall.' Dönitz verified this report with Vizeadmiral Voss, his liaison officer at FHQ, and then ordered Generaloberst Stumpff, Commander-in-Chief, Luftwaffe Reich, to impose a ban on all Luftwaffe flights in the region. Only in captivity did Dönitz hear of the other measures ordered against the Reichsmarschall, particularly the one to shoot him issued on 30 April: 'After our deaths the 23 April traitors are to be shot. Bormann.' From what Göring said in captivity at Bad Mondorf, and the accounts of others in his entourage, I have become convinced that there was in fact no 'high treason' involved. He had been cut off from Hitler, heard the report of Berlin being surrounded, thought Hitler was *hors de combat* and that it was his, Göring's, duty to take action, in accordance with the Reichstag declaration which remained in force and had been confirmed by the secret edict of 29 June 1941. Unfortunately Hitler, who was determined to run the OKW and oversee the relief of Berlin personally by means of the few signals facilities remaining, perceived Göring's offer, made in the seething passion of the time, as high treason, and all the more so since Hitler was still unwilling to acknowledge the adverse verdict of Providence in the matter.

Clarification as to who would be Hitler's successor instead of Göring was yet to come. Dönitz thought it would be Himmler, whose position as the war went on had become the most powerful in the state by virtue of the continual addition to his charge of ever more offices and jobs. Himmler's conduct in the last of the meetings also indicated that he thought of himself as the successor. Particularly striking was a scene I mentioned previously at the situation conference of 27 April at OKW HQ. During these conferences, which were basically for Hitler's benefit, he used to sit at the map table. On this occasion he was absent. Jodl rose and read out his report to the standing circle of listeners. Suddenly, Himmler drew up a chair before the map table and sat down. I considered this very tactless given the impending fall of the Führer. The gesture gave rise to indignation and criticism. Himmler offered Dönitz the chair at his side, for which he thanked him frostily.

Discussing the war situation with the four senior commanders in the North, Dönitz expressed his intention, which he had mentioned once before, that he would keep faith with anybody lawfully appointed by the Führer as his successor in order to avoid 'a tragi-comedy developing out of the present tragedy' as a result of disunity (an expression as I recall coined by Speer). He naturally expected the other gentlemen to follow his lead. During the course of the morning of 30 April, Dönitz received a signal from the Reich Chancellery which had apparently been composed the previous day and was for some reason delayed in transmission. The text read more or less: 'New treason afoot. According to enemy radio Reichsführer had made offer through Sweden to surrender. Führer expects you to act against all traitors lightning fast and steely hard. Bormann.'

This signal put Dönitz in an very awkward position. Was he expected to strike 'lightning fast and steel hard' against Himmler? How should he do that? The only forces he had at his disposal were Kriegsmarine units afloat or in coast defences, none of which were armed or trained for police or army work. Moreover, at this time he had no power of command over the army units at the front in the North. These troops were controlled by Hitler himself through the OKW. The power over the police, SS and the *Ersatzheer* in the interior was exercised by Himmler himself. To remove him forcibly was as good as impossible from the start, and any attempt to do so would most certainly lead to chaos, the avoidance of which Dönitz considered to be one of his most important duties in this situation. Furthermore, he thought that possibly in their isolation, and the prevailing mood of gloom, the Reich Chancellery people might have given the report too much credence. Finally it seemed to him more important to carry out his remaining tasks with due diligence, accepting as few casualties as possible, rather than concentrating his energies on 'traitors'.

He therefore decided to clarify the matter by a personal meeting with Himmler, told me to arrange it at a neutral venue. He met Himmler at about 1500 hrs in the police barracks at Lübeck. Dönitz showed Himmler the signal and asked for his explanation. I was only present during the talk now and again because I was busy drafting the reply to Gauleiter Kaufmann's telex. Dönitz told me later that Himmler denied making any contact with the enemy (see Chapter 12) and claimed that the radio report was a fabrication. He agreed with Dönitz's opinion that whatever happened next, unity was the most thing of all.

Any possibility of Himmler being Hitler's successor was now gone. That he had ever been in the running and the premature revelation of the Count Bernadotte business made Hitler change his mind, I consider unlikely. A widening chasm between the two of them had been perceptible since the failure of the Ardennes Offensive. Dönitz himself stated to his closest circle that day that in view of the impending military disaster, and after Göring and Himmler had been excluded from the succession, he no longer expected any further instructions regarding the matter, nor that there would be a surrender. If that were so, once Hitler was dead he intended to surrender the forces under his command and then seek his own death in battle in order to refute for all time any suspicion of personal cowardice, and by his sacrifice to atone for himself and his men for any stain of betrayal attaching to his independent partial surrender. To what extent Speer influenced Hitler in his decision to appoint Dönitz during his last visit to Berlin on 25 April can no longer be known. It is certain, however, that Dönitz did not know of any part played by Speer in his appointment, and was surprised by the announcement. He found it waiting for him upon his return from Lübeck on 30 April.

Chapter 5

Reich President by Signal

The first report we received about this event reached us at 1835 hrs on 30 April by telegraph. The signal stated:

FRR Grossadmiral Dönitz

In place of the former Reichsmarschall Göring, the Führer had appointed you, Herr Grossadmiral, as his successor. Written full powers follow. With immediate effect you should take all measures which seem appropriate to the present situation. Bormann.

When I placed the signal before Dönitz, Reichsminister Speer was also present, and after a brief silence expressed his best wishes. Given the gravity of the situation, there were no congratulations. It was clear to each of us that this relinquishing of command by the Führer meant at least his imminent death, if it had not already occurred, and a final negative line had been drawn under the heroic and desperate struggle of the German people.

There was never any question as to whether this or later signals which we received were genuine. Weeks previously, following the occupation of large parts of the Reich and the irreparable bombing damage, the whole telephone system began to collapse. This had prompted Dönitz to send mobile naval radio units to the most important areas, including inland, to install the only reliable signals links both to Berlin and the South. A new and unique code was given to each recipient individually to provide the best guarantee of absolute security, or at least to preclude the sending of false messages by unauthorised third parties. Even after the capitulation and especially in captivity, the authenticity of the signals and the succession in law were disputed and doubted, but this was done for tactical reasons. The later discovery of the Führer-Testament removed any basis for these invented doubts.

The signal had been sent from Berlin at 1815 hrs on 30 April, by which time, as we know, Hitler had already been dead since earlier that afternoon. We also know that his Testament was dated 29 April. I would not wish to hazard a guess as to whether the delay in sending it was at his own order, was done deliberately by somebody in his close circle or was due to technical problems in Berlin. Dönitz drew two false conclusions from his appointment:

(1) The Führer was standing down to leave the way clear for the solution which he will not undertake under any circumstances: capitulation.
(2) He had chosen you, a politically untainted soldier, as his successor because the enemy would prefer to negotiate with you.

He inferred from the text of the signal full freedom for himself to negotiate. That same evening, therefore, he summoned the two available bodies, OKW and Reichsführer-SS, to clarify the internal political situation and get control of the Wehrmacht, with which alone it might still be possible to steer future events. On the morning of 1 May a second signal arrived from the Reich Chancellery (sent from Berlin 0740 hrs, arrived Plön HQ 1053 hrs).

FRR Grossadmiral (Chefsache)

Testament in force. I will come to you as soon as possible. Until then my opinion withhold publication. Bormann.

This was our first notification of Hitler's death. As to how and when this death had occurred nothing was said. We thought that Hitler would have taken up arms and fallen in battle. The phrase 'The Führer has fallen' which Dönitz employed at noon that day and later in his address over Norddeutscher Rundfunk that evening were based on this false assumption (Appendix 6 and 7). Dönitz considered the suggestion to withhold publication to be wrong and discounted it from the outset. This was a report which the world, the German people and above all the Wehrmacht had to hear from a German source and not the enemy: the world, in order to clarify who was now the legal head of the Reich: the German people, to inform them himself of the closing of an epoch of such momentous decisions and onerous consequences: and the Wehrmacht in order to prevent the chaos which would inevitably be likely when the commanders and fighting men learned of the death of the man to whom they had sworn an oath of allegiance on the flag, and who now lacked clear guidance as to their future conduct.

On the afternoon of that same 1 May, the signals officer brought me the third and last telegraph message sent from the Reich Chancellery (despatched at 1446 hrs, received 1518 hrs, Appendix 3). The contents of this instruction were apparently taken from the Führer's Testament and bound his successor to comply with it without exception or deviation. However, Dönitz did not feel bound by this order for the following reasons:

1. It directly contradicted the first telegram (1835 hrs, 30 April) in which Dönitz 'with immediate effect should take all measures which seem appropriate to the present situation'.
2. In view of that fact, and the time which had elapsed since Hitler's death – over twenty-four hours – Dönitz doubted that Hitler was the original inspiration for the third signal and did not rule out a conspiracy by Goebbels and Bormann.
3. It was not possible to comply with the last instruction due to the situation.
4. Dönitz's own political ideas for ending the war and forming a successor government did not coincide with this list of Cabinet members. He was determined, on the basis of conscience and being no longer answerable to Hitler, to follow the road which after thorough debate with the men in whom he had confidence seemed the only right one for the welfare of the German people in the present situation.
5. He had already acted as he saw fit and taken initial steps.

Because the publication of the last signal and with it his deviation from the Führer's Testament might have incurred the most unpleasant consequences, and threaten not only his authority but moreover the plan for the orderly ending of the war, Dönitz gave me the signal for safekeeping with the instruction to show it to nobody, not even those closest to him. He discussed it next day with Feldmarschall Keitel and Finance Minister Graf Schwerin von Krosigk, who were both in agreement with his decision. Schwerin in particular pointed out the contradiction which lay in making a person leader of an authoritarian regime but at the same time choosing his Cabinet for him. On 3 May, when Dönitz declared that he would lead a 'Caretaker Reich Government', Schwerin suggested the immediate arrest of Goebbels and Bormann should they surface at Plön contrary to expectations. Dönitz agreed. However, events in Berlin, unknown to us at the time, relieved us of any need to act in this regard.

Chapter 6

The Military Situation on 2 May 1945

In the framework of his memorandum 'Kriegsende 1945' which Dönitz dictated to me in the first weeks of our captivity, he had a concise but comprehensive picture of the military situation at the time of his nomination as head of state. Since it comes from the lop-sided perspective of those days and lacked any documents or maps, from the standpoint of military history it may need some revision of details and a general rounding-off. Nevertheless, and precisely for that reason, it provides the exact picture which the German leadership had of the situation at the time. It was the basis of their decisions and consequently had a decisive influence on the course of events. Since I consider it my duty to represent without reference to later knowledge how developments arose from our contemporary appreciation of the situation, I reproduce Dönitz's memorandum here verbatim:

The military situation of Germany at this time was as follows:

1. The bombing attacks of the final months reduced all war production to its minimum level. There were no reserves of ammunition, weapons or fuel. The road system was totally ruined to the extent that resupplying, or the shipping out of raw materials, completed goods or foodstuffs was extraordinarily difficult, if not impossible.
2. Army Group in Italy had surrendered. The Army in the West under Feldmarschall Kesselring was breaking up.
3. In the East, the South-East Army was in orderly retreat from Yugoslavia. Army Group Rendulic (South) was holding its positions in Austria. Similarly Army Group Schörner (Centre) held a fully intact front against the Russians. The latter two Army Groups had only enough ammunition and fuel for a short period.

4. The intended relief of Berlin had failed. Armee Busse (9.Armee) was attempting to escape encirclement by a retreat to the west. The attack by Armee Wenck (12.Armee) had not broken through and was also in retreat to the west.

5. The Army Group in the northern sector of the Eastern Front (Army Group Vistula) was breaking up as it withdrew into Mecklenburg.

6. The troops in East and West Prussia were under pressure from a greatly superior Russian force. The front in Kurland was holding. Because of the lack of ammunition and fuel they could not be resupplied. The collapse of these fronts was therefore, as with Schörner and Rendulic, merely a matter of time. The Kriegsmarine was attempting to ship out as many troops as possible by sea from Kurland and Prussia.

7. North-west Germany, East Frisia and Schleswig-Holstein had not yet been occupied by the enemy. There were insufficient forces available to hold off the expected attack. The divisions in East Frisia and west of the Elbe were transported to Holstein in an attempt to hold at least this province. That the forces available were too weak for the purpose was demonstrated on 2 May when the enemy, who had crossed the Elbe at Lauenburg, was able to continue his advance immediately to the Baltic coast at Lübeck and Schwerin.

8. Holland, Denmark and Norway together with the Biscay ports, the Channel Islands and Calais were still in German hands. There was no fighting in these areas.

9. Millions of refugees from the civilian population, particularly from North Germany, were fleeing to the West before the advancing Russian front.

10. As the result of air attacks on the ports, and their unflinching continuation of transports to and from Norway and the Baltic, the Kriegsmarine had sustained very heavy losses in surface warships (torpedo boats, minesweepers, S-boats and escort craft). Of the major units only *Prinz Eugen* and *Nürnberg* were still intact.

11. The U-boat arm was on the brink of a revival of the U-boat War once the new types of U-boat began arriving at the front in increasing numbers at the beginning of May.

12. The Luftwaffe had only a small number of aircraft. Operations were extraordinarily restricted by the shortage of fuel and were continuing to decrease.

This overall scenario shows clearly that militarily the war was lost. Since there was also no political possibility of a positive outcome for Germany, as head of state there was nothing left for me to do but end the war as quickly as possible in order to spare further bloodshed.

I have nothing fundamental to add to this account by Dönitz. Yet at this point I believe I should mention a problem which caused feelings to run high before, during and after the capitulation: the scorched-earth policy in Germany.

It is now well-known that scorched-earth policies or lesser forms of the same were not a German invention and had not previously been employed on their own soil. The burning of Moscow, the measures adopted by the Northern states during the American Civil War, the retreat to the Siegfried Line in 1917, the destruction of the French Channel ports in 1940 by the British and the German withdrawal from northern Norway in the autumn of 1944 are just a few examples in which partial or total destruction in special circumstances or through events could be justified.

In the autumn of 1944 the land fighting began to spill over into Reich territory and though regrettable, it seemed essential that the enemy should be hindered by all means possible in his advance and his enjoyment of German means of production for at least as long as a glimmer of hope existed that the situation could be improved. In the view of Dönitz and Jodl, this glimmer of hope no longer existed on 15 March 1945 when, through OKW, Hitler issued his orders for the destruction of all military and economic property. Both therefore tried to moderate the effect of this edict, and at the beginning of April OKW issued 'guidelines' which strictly limited Hitler's original order. Moreover, a number of military and civilian commanders opposed the order directly, but to my knowledge Speer was the only one of them with the courage to tell Hitler what he was doing.

Because the failure to take destructive measures proved very disadvantageous for the German war effort in some cases, and decisively influenced the course of military operations,[1] Dönitz introduced for the Kriegsmarine an order that although preparations were to made to destroy even German ports (blowing up quays, minelaying and blocking navigable channels), the order would only be carried out to the extent that it would serve some immediate military purpose. The measures to destroy the ports of Memel and Gotenhafen (Gdynia/Poland) were executed, but not at Hamburg or the German harbours at the western end of the Baltic.

After we moved up to the coast in the North it was principally Speer, by now constantly in Dönitz's close circle, who reminded him frequently about stopping the destructive measures which he was no longer required to implement. This brought about a further relaxation of the standing order. Once the decision was taken to capitulate, all destructive measures were cancelled.

Chapter 7

Realisation and Decision

Adolf Hitler capitulated on 29 April 1945. Not before the world, but before himself and history. On that day he appointed his successor who received notice on the evening of the following day. Early on 1 May his successor learnt that the Testament was in force.

The military situation was hopeless. The idea fomented by propaganda and many fanatics of 'fighting to the last shell' which would have meant a desperate continuation of the war to the last gasp within and beyond the German frontiers, did not enter Dönitz's thinking. When Berlin fell, the death of Hitler and the occupation of most of the Reich convinced him that the time had come for the German leadership to bear the consequences of their total defeat. He was ready to face up to it himself. Accordingly at the same moment as he assumed full responsibility, he saw it as his primary task to end the war as quickly as possible to spare further pointless sacrifice for friend and foe alike – but in a manner 'worthy of the unique heroic struggle of the German people', and above all to save as many as he could from the horrors of Bolshevism. For this reason the fighting against the Russians had to continue, and no proposals for capitulation were offered to them.[1]

In the West there were two roads available To end hostilities: official capitulation or cessation of resistance. The question whether the latter was more expedient and honourable was considered at length and became the subject of the greatest soul-searching. The bitterness of unconditional surrender and its distressing consequences were known. Admittedly these consequences were to be expected in either case – but could one not avoid the bitter pill of one's own acquiescence by making a last solemn and powerful protest against Fate? Should men continue to fall when a *fait accompli* – total occupation – was imminent? This step might have had some meaning before the armies had bled out, the cities were bombed to rubble and the economy destroyed – now that it would last no more than a few more weeks, should we not stop the sacrifices? Would not the refusal to resist represent a proud and defiant expression before history, into which roots could be set down at some future time? Would not the signing be interpreted as personal cowardice or weakness, the names of the signatories – as had happened once before in living memory – be exposed to the danger of being shamed for all time?

Dönitz experienced all these doubts and wrestled inwardly for the solution. As a personal way out, death would have been the easiest solution. He had nothing more to lose: both sons lost in action in U-boats, his life's work – the U-boat arm – crushed, his estate seized. He dismissed the idea of suicide absolutely, however. He told me once that by this method one easily became tainted by guilt by tacit admission. He felt free of guilt. He had probably considered seeking death in battle before he had been saddled with supreme responsibility, but he desired to atone for only one sin: the surrender of the Kriegsmarine. All considerations of this kind evaporated when by appointment he had the right to decide when the total capitulation should be. He considered this appointment a duty he could not avoid under any circumstances and without regard to his own person. 'I must tread the path which according to my knowledge and conscience seems to be the right one for the people and fighting men, even if its effect is dishonourable or defamatory for me.'

After carefully weighing up the pros and cons he recognised this path to be that of official capitulation led from the top for the following reasons:

(1) *Avoidance of further loss to life and property*
    Losses in battle, destruction by air attacks and the scorched-earth policy could best be prevented by a rapid and immediate surrender.
(2) *Avoidance of chaos*
    To hold off the capitulation, leaving the decision to subordinate officers. Left to the divisional commander, company commander or in the last instance to the individual soldier, this way would necessarily lead to a variety of outcomes. Without doubt in the early days of May 1945 there were men, or whole units (especially of the Waffen-SS and Kriegsmarine), who

placed loyalty and obedience above everything even in the collapse and were prepared to fight to the last breath as their oath of loyalty demanded. The German soldier was trained to do so. The greater the danger for the Fatherland, the more desperately did even the worst of its sons cling to this principle. A patchwork surrender led necessarily to grave altercations down to the smallest grouping, between those in favour of giving up and those who wanted to soldier on, to war between brother and brother, to chaos. The prevention of such an outcome only seemed possible by ordering an end to the fighting and ensuring it was accepted by the fanatics.

(3) *Duty towards the fighting men*

The German soldier swore his oath to the person of Adolf Hitler as 'Führer of the German Reich and People and Supreme Commander of the Wehrmacht'.[2] Even if without doubt it had not been the intention of this personal oath to relieve the defenders of the nation of it if Hitler fell, nevertheless they were formally relieved of it by his death. A new oath to be sworn by every serviceman to the successor was impractical given the confused situation and was not introduced. On the other hand Dönitz did not think he could dispense with this most effective way of binding the armed forces if he wanted to keep them in the palm of his hand and influence events at the front. In his proclamation of 1 May to the armed forces he therefore asserted that the oath sworn to Hitler remained valid.[3] Dönitz did not view the oath as a one-sided means of binding the soldier to the Führer, but rather also as an equally binding obligation on the latter to the fighting services. This implied an obligation to continuously review whether the oath was applicable at any particular time and only to demand its fulfillment if it seemed to him to be justified. The ethos of the concept demanded there be no abuse of the oath. The German Wehrmacht, which had fought heroically for almost six years on all fronts, had a right that the man to whom the oath was sworn also carried out his duty solemnly. He must therefore also relieve the soldier of the most onerous decision – to lay down his weapons – and release him from his oath by capitulating. It was clear to Dönitz that as a result of the collapse, large sections of the Wehrmacht were no longer willing to observe the oath, but he had to spare the 'decent' section of the fighting forces a conflict of conscience.

(4) *Sparing the occupied territories*

Not capitulating would draw the unconquered outposts of the Reich (Norway, Denmark, the Protectorate of Bohemia and Moravia, Holland and a number of enclaves on the French and Mediterranean coasts) into the whirlpool of war. This would create not only a momentary political problem, but also a debt to history. It would cause major resentment for the future relations with these peoples. Whereas they might have some understanding for German measures during the struggle for existence, they would certainly not have sympathy for the Germans having dragged their country to the ramparts needlessly after the war was obviously lost.

(5) *Carrying out the principal aim*

The transports from the East could be only stopped by the military intervention of the Western enemy. The Anglo-American, and not the Soviet, air force, controlled the refugee routes on land and had already contributed to the swift collapse on the Eastern Front. Only the RAF was in a position to effectively restrict the evacuations by sea, which the Russians were attempting in vain to stem. At this time the demarcation line could be sealed off by the Western Powers but not the Russians. Therefore what remained to be done in the East had to be helped by a partial capitulation to the West. The mere proclamation of the 'cessation of the struggle against the West' would not induce the Allies to respond in kind as the events of 28 April had proved. On that day the Wehrmacht Report had announced: 'Our troops on the Elbe have turned their backs to the Americans', but the Americans continued their operations and aerial activities regardless.

(6) *Duties of the victors*

Refusal to capitulate would lengthen the war. The enemy did not want this, and so it gave some margin for us to bargain rather than go immediately for a 'treaty' of unconditional surrender. By bargaining, as Schwerin von Krosigk agreed on 2 May, the treaty of unconditional surrender would then be two-sided.

The victors were not relieved of the requirement to observe and uphold international law, and were on the contrary obliged to do so. The capitulation would be signed only for the German armed forces, not the state, its government or its head. After the laying-down of arms, the state could be deprived of sovereignty, but not its legal claim to it. On the other hand, the existence of state and government were the precondition for negotiations with it under international law, while a capitulation would practically guarantee the recognition of its existence.

Thus the basic question of whether there should be a capitulation was decided, but not how. Since the meeting of Roosevelt and Churchill in Casablanca in January 1943, it was known – and Stalin held to this agreement later – that the Allies would only accept an unconditional surrender on all fronts at the same time. At the armistice all our movements would cease and the fighting forces would be held where they were. This kind of capitulation was rejected during the considerations of 1 May. The terms would be unacceptable because they meant the abandonment of the entire Army in the East, and millions of civilian refugees, to the Russians. It was unfeasible because the Army in the East would never have stood for it. Signing such a document would have been useless, for the new Commander-in-Chief would have had to act in breach of the surrender terms before the ink was dry and as his first act under it. This could provide the enemy with an excuse for reprisals, if he needed one.

Was saving the Army in the East and the refugees worth fighting on for? Did the people from the fertile farming lands of the Eastern zone with their better living conditions expect something better than the overcrowded, bomb-ruined West, to which they had always exported foodstuffs in the past? Was the psychosis to flee, which had seized the people and fighting men in the East, perhaps only the result of a cruel propaganda hoax, overtaken by events, and to which we too had fallen victim? Dönitz had checked and spoken of it on various occasions. There could be no doubt as to the reliability of the reports from the regions already occupied by the Soviets. Far too many had seen at first hand or themselves been subjected to unimaginable atrocities committed by the Russians on their arrival. After visiting the front and contacting the endless streams of refugees during his tours over the last few weeks Dönitz had become convinced: the panic had not been created artificially but had its roots principally in the criminality of the Soviet enemy, strangers to humanity. Everybody now followed one rule: Do not fall into Russian hands! Being taken prisoner seemed an especially harrowing fate under these circumstances. An immediate total surrender was therefore, as Dönitz had said frequently, 'Treason against the troops on the Eastern Front.' For this reason he thought the only way both possible and right to end the war quickly was to pull back the Eastern Front to the known demarcation line while saving as many lives as possible. This would require at least eight to ten days. At the same time he would continue with the evacuations by sea with anything capable of sailing.

In the West, on the other hand, he would attempt to obtain partial surrenders to cease hostilities and only continue fighting while it remained necessary to achieve the main aim. Here he was thinking of only a small sector of the front, along the Elbe from Lauenburg to Hamburg to keep open the last remaining 'gate' for the refugees from Pomerania, Mecklenburg and Brandenburg. Dönitz made these intentions clear in his radio broadcast to the German people on the evening of 1 May (Appendix 7).

Bearing in mind these aims, it was decided also that the attempts to obtain partial surrender terms had to be made cautiously and must not be made public lest the Russians understand what was afoot and stop them. It would be best therefore to approach only Montgomery at first, and not the more politically handcuffed Eisenhower. Contact was to be made by Feldmarschall Busch. Without his agreement, lower levels were already talking to the enemy. Strict wireless silence was imposed in order not to arouse Russian suspicions.

Of especial importance for success was the personality of the negotiator. Because the suggestions made by OKW did not meet with Dönitz's approval, although Army units were mainly involved he decided to speak to the newly appointed Commander-in-Chief, Kriegsmarine, Generaladmiral von Friedeburg, and informed him during 1 May of his ideas and how he proposed to carry them through.

This was the overall situation and our plan on the evening of 1 May 1945. It received a rapid, exciting impulse through the events of the following day, but was finally ended by the stonewalling of Eisenhower, although not before its objective had been partially achieved.

Chapter 8

Partial Capitulation in the North

During 2 May we learnt from radio broadcasts and a telex from Feldmarschall Kesselring that a few days earlier the Army in Italy had secretly signed a surrender (Army Group South-West, Generaloberst von Vietinghoff). It came into effect at 1400 hrs. This to all intents and purposes initiated the final collapse of the German military fronts and was the first public admission of a surrender. As it occurred at a moment that Dönitz considered premature, with regard to his own plan to end the war, initially he was not in agreement with it. The Army Group had acted independently against standing orders, and this independence more or less, if not actually, coincided with his appointment as Supreme Commander, causing him to fear a rapid escalation in indiscipline on other fronts. As a result of further events that day, and a situation report telexed by Kesselring covering von Vietinghoff's back retrospectively, Dönitz then took the view that he should consider this an isolated incident and not incorporate it into his plan to end the war.

In the North, the initiative to begin capitulation negotiations was spurred by the Western enemy on 2 May. That day, British forces broke out from their bridgehead at Lauenburg and made a quick thrust to Lübeck, while the Americans crossed the Elbe further down and, meeting no opposition, reached the Baltic at Wismar. This latter action came as a complete surprise to the German commanders, who had not reckoned on an advance crossing the demarcation line into the Russian zone and thus had made no serious attempt to defend it because all conquests of territory from the West were considered salvation from the Soviets. The British advance had been expected, however. An attempt had been made to halt it using the last weak forces under Generalfeldmarschall Busch because the retreat from Mecklenburg to Holstein was still under way.

The manner in which we learned of the British advance was typical of the confusion in communications at that time. The situation conference was held at 1600 hrs in the Grossadmiral's study in our barracks hut at Plön. Jodl reported: 'Early this morning the British left their Lauenburg bridgehead and advanced. Feldmarschall Busch is hopeful that he can hold the front for a few days more …' At the same moment I was speaking on the telephone with the Draeger works at Lübeck on another matter. I was surprised when the person at the other end began shouting into the instrument, and upon my request that he should lower his voice he shouted back: 'I can't understand a word you're saying, there's such a racket in the streets, one tank after another is rolling past … yes, all British – do you want to listen?' and turned the receiver towards the street so that I could hear the clanking of the tracks more clearly.

The last gate between East and West was now double-barred. The fighting against the West, the only purpose of which had been to keep this door open, was now senseless. Dönitz drew the necessary inference immediately and set his plan in motion as soon as he heard my report:

1. Begin partial surrender negotiations immediately according to the plan.
2. Transfer HQ to Flensburg.

The latter measure was essential to maintain the OKW and Government's freedom to manouevre in the coming talks for as long as possible. Plön was now unsuitable because it was only an hour from Lübeck by tank, and the British could be expected at any moment. Dönitz telephoned von Friedeburg and informed him that the plan was in effect. They met for closer consultation on the Leversauer suspension bridge over the Kiel Canal, which Friedeburg crossed on his drive west, and Dönitz to the north. They met at 2100 hrs after a delay due to causes mentioned below.

The instructions to von Friedeburg corresponded to those set out in the preceding chapter: a partial, purely military capitulation in the entire continental north-west, but if possible without prejudice to the movements from the East on land and sea. In order to make von Friedeburg fully acquainted with Dönitz's thinking, Konteradmiral Wagner from Dönitz's personal staff, General Kinzel, head of Command Staff North and three other officers accompanied him. The announcement of this delegation to the British 21st Army Group and permission to pass through the front were negotiated by the military commandant of Hamburg on the instructions of OKW (Appendix 8).

After this conversation we drove on to the new and final HQ of the German leadership. It was our last experience of war. Our start had been delayed by extremely intrusive enemy fighter-bomber activity. Close to our barrack hut at Plön our own vehicles and some Swedish coaches clearly bearing neutrality markings were destroyed by low-flying aircraft. Dönitz, Schwerin von Krosigk and I now set off for Flensburg in our 5-tonne armoured Mercedes limousine. The car had been a gift from Hitler with instructions that we were to use it. It was proof against assassination attempts, but not machine-gunning from the air, and we were forever stopping and leaping out. Not until 0300 hrs did we reach our destination. The base commander, Kapitän zur See Lüth, escorted us to the large passenger ship *Patria*, now used as a floating hostel. I remember having sailed past her aboard a destroyer during the 1938 Naval Review at Kiel when Hitler and the Hungarian Vice-regent Admiral Horthy had been aboard her.

Dönitz went to rest. After briefly greeting the Reich Minister for the Occupied Eastern Territories, Alfred Rosenberg, I used these quiet hours of the day when I was off duty to look over our new 'HQ'. In contrast to Plön the appointments were meagre and by no means self-contained. The barrack huts for the Command Staff were only partially equipped and the signals arrangements hopelessly inadequate. Lüth therefore offered his own base command building and installed facilities for Dönitz, the Government and OKW in feverish haste. We dubbed the building 'Wilhelmstrasse'.

When I returned to the *Patria* at 0530 hrs, I found Dönitz in a state of disquiet. He had been notified of a series of rumours that the British were on the move again in the north-west, and he had not been able to obtain clear reports or send his orders to the competent commanders. All he could do was set up a last defence line on the Kiel Canal to prevent the British crossing from the south, which would enable them to put us out of action while the envoys were still talking to them. In the course of the day we discovered that the rumours were exaggerated. The defence of the Kiel Canal was now properly organised, but 'Sea-Fort Kiel', adequately armed to ward off an attack, was declared an open city. Finally, 3 May mainly served in Flensburg for talks with the Reich Commissioners and Wehrmacht commanders of the foreign territories still occupied by German forces. I have described these later. On the whole these talks confirmed the correctness of the chosen path of capitulation.

* * *

Towards midnight, von Friedeburg returned and made a short report to Dönitz. He had been delayed on the outward journey by a traffic accident and had not arrived in Hamburg until the early morning of 3 May, behind schedule. Gauleiter Kaufmann, in whose command post his reception was one of icy reserve and suspicion, had failed to appear. The party had had to drive off immediately in order to reach the frontline crossing-point at the time agreed by the Hamburg military commandant. Unfortunately we had over-looked the need for an interpreter, which had proved a handicap in the talks.

Their reception and treatment by the British was correct except for a humiliating ceremony in which a stick was laid on the ground to mark where the German negotiators were to line up to await the appearance of Montgomery.[1] This frosty beginning did not harm the talks, however. At 0900 hrs on 4 May discussions were held at Flensburg about the conditions Montgomery wanted to impose. Present were Dönitz. Schwerin, Keitel, Jodl, von Friedeburg and Oberstleutnant Brudermüller, Jodl's adjutant. The agree-ment encompassed what had been sought in the earlier chapter 'Partial Capitulation in the North', but went further to include Holland, Denmark and the German fleet within the area of the surrender. These last two demands appeared to be against the general aim, the saving of the people in the East.

Von Friedeburg calmed Dönitz's fears by assuring him that he had been told the evacuation transports could continue to run and that individual sol-diers who wished to surrender at the demarcation line would be taken as British prisoners. Montgomery declined to discuss the question of the civilian refugees. As to the surrender of Holland and Denmark there was mutual agreement because a peaceable transfer prevented the danger of insurrection and took both countries out of the war, contrary to our inclination the previous day.

An argument developed over the demand that military material should not be destroyed. This meant handing over intact all weapons in the north-west, and hit Dönitz particularly hard as respects the Kriegsmarine units, since he had been the greatest and most visible exponent of German naval warfare. Keitel and Jodl both thought that this clause could not be reconciled with German military honour and suggested that destruction should begin at once. Schwerin opposed the idea since it could void the treaty. Montgomery would consider himself no longer bound by it, and he could consider reprisals and even stop the reception of Germans coming in from the East. By such a clear breach of the treaty as his first measure in government, Dönitz would lose all credibility as a negotiating partner. We did not know what might be the enemy's true intentions, but we could not allow the possibility of the project being throttled at birth.

My objection: The treaty came into force at 0800 hrs on 5 May: we should fight on until then, during which time the weapons could be destroyed. Von Friedeburg overrode this: by the letter of the agreement it was a way round but it struck at the verbally agreed spirit of the accord. With heavy heart Dönitz decided to accept the demand, knowing that as supreme warlord he alone carried the responsibility before German history. By surrendering his weapons intact contrary to military tradition, he shouldered the guilt. Having reported a dignified procedure for the surrender and honourable treatment for prisoners of war, von Friedeburg received full authority to sign the instrument and flew back to the British. At 1940 hrs the same evening we received a signal confirming the signing at Montgomery's HQ (Appendix 11 and 12) and at 0800 hrs on 5 May the guns fell silent. Following Dönitz's order, OKW ordered that no weapons were to be destroyed and with a brief explanation ordered them to be surrendered to the enemy (Appendix 12 and 13).

It was obeyed almost without exception, a sign not of indifference, but of astonishing discipline to the last moment. How onerous the leadership and armed forces found this order was evidenced by the number of requests for confirmation and the various signals with which a number of units signed off. Only the U-boat arm, loyal to Dönitz in a special way, declined the order in the Homeland. Dönitz had already left when Fregattenkapitän Liebe and Oberleutnant zur See Duppel, both veteran U-boat commanders, stormed into my office. Both were attached to BdU Staff that had transferred to Flensburg with us, but the Chief of Staff and his No 1 Admiral Staff Officer had already flown to Norway to direct operations there as required. Liebe and Duppel had now received the incomprehensible order not to scuttle the U-boat fleet. They would only obey this order if they heard it from Dönitz's own mouth. I was certain that after the previous conversations, Dönitz would not go back on his decision. I was also sure that in his heart he was as much against the surrender of the U-boat fleet to the enemy as I was. Therefore I refused them an interview with Dönitz with the observation that I knew what I would do as a commander. Both understood.

The secret codeword to scuttle the boat kept by the signals staff aboard each U-boat was 'Regenbogen'. To send this by signal *en clair* as required was not possible and would in any case have been retracted officially at once. U-boats that received the order by other means in the North Sea and Baltic ports were scuttled on the night of 4 May. In some cases crewmen died voluntarily aboard their boats. Dönitz himself was at first very surprised by the mass scuttling and on 5 May called for a full report on the previous night's events from the senior U-boat commander at each location. None of the feared reprisals followed. On the contrary, we later gained the impression that this destruction was approved by the Western Allies, so that in the later three-way split of naval vessels the Russians would receive very few submarines, and none of the new U-boat types fell into their hands.

Chapter 9

Unconditional Surrender

On 3 May 1945, Feldmarschall Kesselring received a signal giving him freedom to capitulate to the Western Allies. On the 5th, at Kesselring's request, Generaloberst Löhr was also given express permission to negotiate with Field Marshal Alexander. Löhr hoped this would lead to the Western Allies occupying Austria. As to what happened next we then remained ignorant. Decisive for moving matters forward, however, was the second mission of Generaladmiral von Friedeburg. In the previously described meeting early on 4 May he had been instructed that after signing the cease-fire with Montgomery, he should then see Eisenhower to obtain a partial, purely military capitulation with regard to US forces on a similar basis. The hope for success with Eisenhower was based on the two previous partial surrenders obtained with the British in Northern Italy and north-west Germany.

Before Dönitz had received news of how von Friedeburg had fared, although under no pressure from the enemy he ordered a number of measures which bear witness to his decision to end the war wherever possible and prevent further senseless bloodshed. On 4 May he ordered an end to the U-boat War (Appendix 10) although he was not bound by any agreement to do so as regards U-boats away from the north-west of Germany. On 5 May he cancelled *Werwolf*, the underground resistance movement brought into being a few weeks previously, since he considered it counter-productive in the West if it was being run at the same time as attempts to cease hostilities.

At 0900 hrs on 6 May we were informed on the progress of von Friedeburg's negotiations at Eisenhower's HQ by General Kinzel, who had been left back with Montgomery, for whom he was acting as a despatch runner because of the agreed radio silence. Dönitz summoned Keitel, Jodl, Schwerin and Wegener to hear Kinzel's report, after which there was a discussion. Von Friedeburg advised that Eisenhower was not prepared to concede a partial capitulation under any circumstances. He was insisting on an immediate, simultaneous unconditional surrender on all fronts. German troops would remain in their present positions, the sinking or sabotaging of naval vessels, aircraft and other equipment was forbidden with immediate effect. OKW would be responsible for ensuring that these terms were observed, or punitive measures would ensue.

In the discussion all participants considered the terms unacceptable because they meant abandoning the German armies in the East to the Russians. Moreover it was felt that no soldier on the Eastern Front would 'lay down his arms and stay where he was'. On the other hand, the hopeless situation, the danger of further heavy casualties for ourselves in the West and the certainty of an unavoidable collapse in the short term begged a solution even for the intact armies. Since no way out of the dilemma could be thought of, it was agreed to put matters before Eisenhower with absolute frankness. Jodl was given the job and went to Allied HQ with full powers to offer unconditional surrender to the West, but not the East. Since there were some doubts about the mission's chances of success, Dönitz gave Jodl an additional full written authority to sign a military capitulation on all fronts. The showing of this document, and any action based on it, were dependent on Dönitz's consent by telegraphic signal beforehand.

Jodl's mission did not achieve the hoped-for success. At 0015 hrs on 7 May Dönitz received Jodl's signal from Allied HQ sent at 2145 hrs on the 6th. This read:

> General Eisenhower insists that we sign today. If not the Allied front lines will be shut to those persons attempting to surrender individually, and all negotiations will be broken off. I see no other options but signature or chaos. Request immediate wirelessed confirmation whether I have the full authority to sign the capitulation. The capitulation can then come into force. Hostilities will cease on 9 May at 0000 hrs German summer time. Jodl.

By this he meant 0001 hrs on 9 May. I made brief notes about the debate on this ominous signal by the decision-makers at German HQ:

1. Eisenhower's stance is absolute blackmail, as he is threatening to hand over all Germans east of his lines to the Russians if we refuse.
2. Generaloberst Jodl, who earlier had been very opposed to the total capitulation because it was impossible to carry through completely, must have further grim reasons if he now believes it is the only way out.
3. By setting the date for midnight on 8 May we have won forty-eight hours time, which will make it possible to save at least the major part of the troops in the East.

Jodl then received the agreed full authority by signal and signed the unconditional surrender of the German forces on land, sea and in the air in all theatres of war at 0241 hrs on 7 May 1945 in Eisenhower's HQ at Rheims.

At 1055 hrs the same day we were in receipt of the exact terms of the capitulation. They were transmitted by signal and cable to all units of the Wehrmacht throughout the world. Couriers were despatched by Dönitz to commanders in far-flung outposts to explain their necessity and request the loyal observance of the conditions in the interests of the German people. At 1245 hrs, Schwerin von Krosigk proclaimed the armistice to the German people over Flensburg Radio to pre-empt their hearing it from the enemy (Appendix 19). At 1600 hrs, Jodl returned to deliver his personal report on the unbending, very brusque attitude of Eisenhower whom he considered a stark contrast to the understanding ways of his Chief of Staff Walter B. Smith. After long talks with the latter he had perceived some hope of avoiding surrendering in the East, but this had been crushed by the terse intervention of Eisenhower with his ultimatum.

The presumed 'further grim reasons' (see my Point 2 above) which caused Jodl to accept the terms were confirmed thus: besides shutting down the front line, Eisenhower had threatened to resume the terror bombing of German cities in the north, even though the treaty with the British had been in force for thirty-six hours and the cease-fire was in effect, with the observation thatas far as he was concerned Montgomery did not speak for the U.S. Air Force.

On 8 May, on instructions from Eisenhower, which had probably been demanded by the Russians and which he had forced Jodl to accept as a condition at Rheims, there was to be a second surrender ceremony at Berlin-Karlshorst. Since the unconditional surrender was already in force once Jodl signed the instrument on 7 May, this second performance in Berlin was considered to be a pantomime. As ordered, Generalfeldmarschall Keitel, Generaladmiral von Friedeburg and Generaloberst Stumpff, deputising for the wounded Luftwaffe Commander-in-Chief Ritter von Greim, turned out to fulfill this pathetic obligation. Following the script, the German actors all had to present their authority as plenipotentiaries duly signed by Dönitz (Appendix 15). These were examined closely to ensure they were in order and then accepted. This public recognition of the person of Grossadmiral Dönitz as Commander-in-Chief of the Wehrmacht also implied that the Allies recognised him as head of state, since both offices were linked and a ready separation of the functions could not be readily engineered.

The German delegation, which was only there expressly to 'ratify' the already signed-for conditions, wondered – despite the good food – how long they would have to wait for the performance to begin, and assumed that the delay was due to extended celebrations. Late that afternoon a Russian colonel came with the news that there were certain modifications to the text of the Rheims version. They wanted the German delegation to look them over and say if they would still be prepared to sign. Since in the opinion of the German officers the changes did not modify the purely military nature of the capitulation, Keitel gave them the nod. After a few more hours' wait the English, German and Russian language copies were signed. Contrary to the date on each instrument, the signing occurred at 0016 hrs on 9 May. Fifteen minutes earlier the capitulation had come into effect on all fronts on the basis of the true document of Rheims.

In Kurland and on the Channel coast, in Norway and Crete, in the Reich and on the high seas, the last German soldiers laid down their arms. The Wehrmacht's struggle was over. The vast majority had believed in the rightness of the German cause and – the longer it went on – fought out of despairing necessity. The outcome was total defeat and misery for the Fatherland, for whose welfare they had believed themselves to be fighting. The Wehrmacht Report of 8 May (Appendix 20), and the last Orders of the Day to the forces, sought to do justice to the terrible tragedy, a mismatch of hope and reality, intention and result, and to give the purely military events at least some degree of dignified closure.

As predicted, the order to capitulate was not observed on the Eastern Front where it was thought there was still a chance of reaching the West. These attempts led to serious incidents, particularly in the former Protectorate of Bohemia. Beforehand, Feldmarschall Schörner had informed the courier bringing him the capitulation order that due to Czech resistance the communications system had been largely destroyed and it was no longer possible to direct operations from Division. There was bound to be independent action by subordinate formations. This report coincided with Dönitz's secret instructions, which the courier had also brought, to allow German troops to continue to make for the West after the capitulation came into effect. When Eisenhower protested, he was answered by reference to Jodl's argument of 6 May. Feverish use had been made of the forty-five hours between signing the surrender and its coming into effect along all parts of the Eastern Front, which Jodl had crafted with the 'poor communications network' excuse. These delaying tactics over the nine days between the appointment of Dönitz and the final laying down of arms enabled between two-and-a-half and three million people to be saved from the Russians. In particular the remains of General Busse's army from Silesia, General Wenck's army from Brandenburg and Generaloberst Heinrici's Army Group from Pomerania were brought across the Elbe and Elbe-Trave Canal almost intact, while large contingents of Army Groups Centre (Generalfeldmarschall Schörner) and South (Generaloberst Rendulic) fought through to the West. Until the last moment, the Kriegsmarine and mercantile marine ran an unceasing shuttle service bringing out refugees from Pomerania and Prussian ports and troops from Kurland for the West aboard dangerously overloaded vessels.[1] The port of Libau was exposed to constant Russian air attack, and due to the limited capacity on the quays only a fraction of the brave defenders of Kurland could be brought out. From many conversations I inferred that this army appeared to reflect the fate of its Supreme Commander-in-Chief, sacrificing itself to the pressure of the victor and events.

The circumstances surrounding the capitulation of the German Wehrmacht have not so far [1964. Tr] undergone exhaustive enquiry, yet it is precisely the 'unconditional' capitulation that led to the most grave consequences. The comprehensive changes to the structure and shape of Germany that the victors felt justified or obliged to make, are without doubt the de facto consequence of the military collapse of the Third Reich. Equally without doubt the legal basis for these measures is not to be found in the 'Instrument of Military Surrender' (Appendix 14 and 16). This instrument, as can be seen from the text and signatories, is exclusively concerned with the Wehrmacht. No representative of the German government was present at the negotiations nor was one requested by the Allied Commander-in-Chief, who talks of 'a capitulation of the German government' in his memoirs. On the contrary, Clause 4 of the instrument of surrender expressly stipulates that this instrument of surrender is without prejudice to general conditions of surrender, which at some later time 'might be imposed on Germany and the German Wehrmacht'. Such conditions were never subsequently been brought to the attention of that German government, nor acknowledged by it, nor was anything ever signed to that effect while that German government existed.

It was not until after the removal by force of the Caretaker Government of the Reich on 23 May 1945 that the victors made a unilateral declaration of Germany's capitulation (Appendix 26). Neither Dönitz and his government nor Jodl, who signed the instrument of military surrender, were consulted on the matter. The day when suspicion was aroused that the Allies were proposing to abuse the actual surrender terms was 7 July 1945 when Colonel Andrus, U.S. commandant of our prison at Bad Mondorf, announced that 'The German State has ceased to exist'. In the face of uproar, the colonel corrected himself and said that the sentence should read, 'The German Government has ceased to exist'. This formula was also objected to, lacking legality as it did because it had been achieved by the use of brute force. Dönitz therefore seized the statement as the opportunity to set forth his views for posterity on the character and extent of the capitulation. I delivered this declaration in German and English versions at the official request of the prison governor. I managed to retain the original draft, which bears minor corrections in Dönitz's own hand, through all seven stations of my captivity and have included the text as Appendix 28.

Chapter 10

The Fate of the Occupied Territories

At the time when Dönitz took over the affairs of the Reich on 1 May 1945, the foreign 'possessions' still in German hands were Denmark, Norway as far as Lyngenfjord, most of Holland and the Protectorate of Bohemia and Moravia. A few small enclaves on the Channel coast, Biscay and in the Aegean had no further significance and were therefore left out of consideration. The discussion on the main areas addressed the following questions:

1. Do these territories have any military or political value in German hands that might be useful in the coming negotiations?
2. Should the German government and military leadership attempt to extend their freedom to manoeuvre and negotiate by using these foreign possessions and, if so, which ones?
3. What is the best way to hand over these territories at the surrender?

Since Dönitz did not want to resolve these questions without consulting the competent military and political men responsible for the territories, and also wanted to ensure that none of them would 'revolt' following the change of leader and continue the war on his own account, he wirelessed signals summoning the military and civilian commandants of each of the four territories. The talks were held on 3 and 4 May with each commandant separately in the presence of Dönitz, Schwerin, Wegener, Keitel and Jodl, and occasionally Himmler and Speer. In general, the following facts were established and decisions made:

1. The possessions still in German hands have no political value. None of the victors would be ready to make concessions for a territory which would have to be given up within a week or so anyway (except Himmler, who

spoke of them being 'in pawn'). Nevertheless, no stone could be left unturned in the quest to improve the German negotiating position.

2. Dönitz categorically rejected the idea of flying over Norway, Denmark or the Protectorate with the Government and OKW on a kind of 'showing the flag' exercise. This he considered unworthy and pointless because it meant extending the war uselessly, promised Germany no advantages and could bring the chosen territory additional misfortune.

3. He laid great value on these territories being spared any further fury of war and thought an attempt should be made to surrender them in the most advantageous way possible in the hope that it might gain some credit for Germany in the future. Any provocation of the native population was to be avoided, and power relinquished as smoothly as possible. As regards supply and other public functions, all possible aid and assistance was to be given. It was our duty to maintain order and keep the peace as long as the responsibility remained in our hands, and to avoid unforeseeable and dis-advantageous consequences for both sides in the event of major distur-bances being fomented.

Beside these general points of view covering all areas discussed, the talks touched on, and made decisions regarding, the following individual problems:

Bohemia and Moravia
(Reich Protector Frank: Generalleutnant von Natzmer, Chief of Staff, Army Group Centre, appointed his deputy by Schörner).

Politically, this region was almost lost. Bohemia was on the verge of revolu-tion. The solution seemed to be to keep it subjected to a degree of German influence. We had no information as to what had been agreed by the Allies at Yalta with respect to the region. One had to assume that the intention was to liberate it. There were upper class Czech groups with who he, Frank, was in contact who saw great danger in such a development and would certainly prefer their country to be liberated by the Western Powers. One should there-fore attempt to arrange a surrender to the Americans with the assistance of Czech politicians.

Neither Dönitz nor Schwerin thought much of this idea because it might aim to change the accord between the Allies and thus lead to tensions. It would not hurt to take soundings, however, which Frank was asked to handle. If successful, it might relieve Dönitz of the major headache he had regarding the existing German forces there. It was decided to declare Prague an open city, however, and so give the population peace of mind.

Subsequently we were unable to discover what steps if any Frank undertook: on the morning of 6 May we heard of the Prague Uprising and all further contact with the Reich Protectorate HQ was lost. From a military point of view the Protectorate was held by Army Group Centre, said to be intact, and which held a very strong natural defensive line in the Sudetenland, but could only hold on until its current provisions and supplies ran out. This was expected in about three weeks. Already on 1 May Dönitz was talking of abandoning the Sudetenland and moving the front westwards towards the American lines to avoid having the bulk of the Army Group fall into Russian hands at the surrender. He was dissuaded by OKW and Generalleutnant Natzmer on the grounds that the army would break up if the Sudetenland were abandoned. Experience showed that a withdrawal tended to be more orderly if the troops were forced back by the enemy that if they left an area at their own volition under no pressure. This was the correct decision but the collapse of the Army Group occurred anyway a few days later and valuable time was lost in which many more soldiers could have been saved from Russian captivity. Nevertheless, on 4 May Dönitz insisted that preparations for an immediate evacuation to the West must be taken in hand, and the order to move out was issued on 6 May. That morning, Lieutenant-Colonel W. [*sic*] of Montgomery's Staff spoke with the Grossadmiral personally and recommended the immediate retreat of the Schörner front.

Holland
(Reich Commissioner Seyss-Inquart)

In this area certain agreements existed with the enemy that had helped improve the food situation for the populace. In line with general policy it was decided to offer a partial surrender. Seyss-Inquart doubted whether this would succeed because of the 1943 Casablanca Agreement. Dönitz ordered that hostilities should continue until any cease-fire came into effect, but there should be no scorched-earth measures or flooding.

At Montgomery's insistence, which coincided with later German intentions, Holland was included in the partial capitulation that came into effect at 0800 hrs on 5 May. This meant there was nothing further for the territorial governor to do. Seyss-Inquart appeared reflective and clear-thinking, and made no attempt to escape his responsibilities. He was confined involuntarily to HQ for several days because the S-boat that brought him could not put out because of the weather, the only link between Flensburg and Holland being by sea.

Denmark
(Reich Plenipotentiary for Denmark Dr Best: Generaloberst Lindemann)

Despite a growing resistance movement, the political situation was still secure. The danger of insurrection was only feared from the intervention of foreigners. The refugee transports were heightening tension since they guaranteed that the war would continue on Danish soil to the last moment.

The military situation was favourable. The country was easy to hold and well supplied. The fighting strength and morale of the military units was unbroken. One of the common soldiers present, overjoyed at hearing the echo of his own oft-repeated opinions, declared: 'I guarantee the men, and order generally in the country: no signs of landings – therefore come to North Schleswig, Herr Grossadmiral, and we shall close the bottleneck and make the last decent stand of the war.' Schwerin stopped the overzealous soldier: 'What for, Herr General?' Denmark was included in the surrender to Montgomery and this relieved Dönitz of any further concerns in the area.

Norway
(Reich Commissioner Terboven: General der Artillerie Böhme)

The political situation here was favourable for the moment. The German collapse and the imminent end of the war were generally expected, and since everybody wanted to survive it with no further bloodshed there was little last-minute enthusiasm for an uprising. The region had been well supplied for some considerable time: the Commander-in-Chief was convinced that his troops were well able to defend Norway. These favourable factors, together with the inaccessible and easily defended terrain, invited a 'heroic resistance', and Dönitz was all the more anxious that there should be no pockets of resistance and that the transfer of power should proceed without a hitch.

In this respect Himmler admitted that he had put out feelers in Sweden for a capitulation. He thought it was both possible and right to offer the surrender of Norway to the Swedes so that their 'brethren could arrive as liberators'. This political gesture promised that the German army in Norway could be interned in Sweden instead of being taken prisoner. Gruppenführer Schellenberg, head of Overseas SD, was making the necessary contacts and had got the train on the rails. He would handle the negotiations himself.

Dönitz's fears that Sweden might be pressured by the Russians to hand over these soldiers were dispelled by Schwerin. If Sweden accepted their surrender, which he doubted, they would only do so with British approval. Dönitz thereupon agreed to the approaches but did not provide Schellenberg with written authority to conclude a treaty. He wanted to reserve the right to decide for himself and not until he had received a telephoned report on the progress of the talks. The whole business seemed very vague to him and might invite a major political disaster. As it happened, Schellenberg's mission achieved no practical results and was overtaken by events.

* * *

For the sake of completeness I think I should present my personal impressions of the Reich governors of those countries. With the exception of Terboven, who followed the proceedings with a cold eye and only took part now and again, all of them seemed to have the fate of their own particular territory at heart. None had a guilty conscience, none was worried about being put on trial or exposed to the wrath of an oppressed people. All of them wanted to stay in their posts in order to personally oversee the German surrender and departure. None of them made an attempt to avoid his responsibility and save his own skin by fleeing. Even though Himmler took this way out, Frank or Dr Best would have needed it to have had excellent prospects for success to have followed him.

I cannot really allow myself to make a judgment on the activities of the Reich governors and the Wehrmacht commandants in the occupied territories. I have no way of measuring the extent of the guilt they incurred, if any. I would not wish to decide what measures were their own or Hitler's, or which were forced upon them by the harsh necessities of war. Even if they had blood on their hands as a result of many acts or omissions, I have to respect their personal demeanour in the days of the collapse.

Chapter 11

The Unpolitical Cabinet

Before making important decisions and after receiving portentous news, Dönitz would go outside for a period of reflection. Shortly after the surprise of his appointment as head of state on the evening of 30 April, he took me for a walk with his dogs, the guard detachment following behind. After a long silence he asked suddenly, 'What type of State do you think is best?'

Even today I am not convinced that one can answer this question simply by saying 'Monarchy', 'Democracy' or 'Dictatorship' – or at least not until one has obtained some definition of what the terms imply. Therefore I remained silent. Dönitz only asked in order to develop his own line of thought. He did not think that the military way, to which he had been subject all his life as a serviceman, was satisfactory for governing a state because success depended so heavily on the personality of the administrator of state power. Therefore this form came with too many dangers for country and people if the 'Führer' or his appointees had their own agenda. He thought that the dualist system we had had at the start of the Nazi regime, in which there was 'a Chancellor who acted and a state President who restrained him', both being accountable to Parliament and people, was the best solution.

After this brief digression into political philosophy he returned to a sober consideration of the facts. 'In a short while I have to contact the enemy. The Foreign Minister, under whose aegis we became embroiled in this war – and immaterial of whatever guilt might attach to him – is not the right man for the job. For the post I need a personality who has some standing abroad. Find out where the former Reich Foreign Minister von Neurath is.'

After unsuccessful attempts to locate him, on 1 May I called Ribbentrop's military adjutant. He did not know where Neurath was either and asked his chief. I waited on the telephone until Ribbentrop answered and wanted to know why we needed the address. I gave an evasive answer and he asked for a personal meeting with Dönitz. Late that evening he received Dönitz and had it out with him. Why was he looking round for a new Foreign Minister? Dönitz explained and asked for Ribbentrop's suggestions. He promised to think it over, but reported next day there was no better candidate than himself.

Dönitz now invited Reich Minister Graf Schwerin von Krosigk, who had also come to the North, for a talk. The two men knew each other only from a conference a few days earlier in Plön. The night drive from Plön to Flensburg on 3 May had given them a further opportunity for a detailed exchange of views. Schwerin von Krosigk hesitated to accept the office of Foreign Minister that he was offered but finally accepted it as a duty he could not escape. No personal ambition was involved. Dönitz often said later how fortunate he had been in this choice. He had now discussed all questions aris-ing and the decisions to be made. Their shared viewpoint and deep aware-ness of their responsibilities led to harmonious cooperation. Both agreed that the lost war should be ended as soon as possible accompanied by the saving of the greatest possible number of Germans from Bolshevism, that they should take the difficult path of capitulation, and how this should be handled. They would have to wait and see if the enemy would recognise and co-oper-ate with them, while obviously cutting off all party-political ties. Only purely technically expert ministers should remain in the Cabinet. For this reason it was called 'the Unpolitical Cabinet'.

In order to give the new head of state a free hand in the choice of his col-leagues, the ministers of the old Reich Government in the North were dis-charged on the evening of 2 May but asked to remain at the disposal of the Grossadmiral in case he should need them. Dönitz was initially undecided whether a formal government was advisable or even necessary. He had no illusions as to its likely term of office and sphere of influence. He did not believe that any of the victor states, and certainly not all four together, would allow a government which had come forth either directly or indirectly from the Nazi regime to remain in office. As full power was bound to pass into the hands of the enemy in the as yet unoccupied parts of Germany within the next few days, his own task as he saw it was simply to help bring this about. He toyed with the idea of having no Cabinet at all, and proceeding with a

Foreign Minister alone, but it soon became clear that the other Cabinet port-folios should be filled. The grounds for this were both idealistic and practical in nature:

1. It seemed advisable to replace the Government stipulated in the Testament by Hitler and advised to us in extracts (see signal 1446 hrs on 1 May 1945, Appendix 5) before the publication of the Testament, lest Goebbels or Bormann should suddenly turn up and sow confusion.
2. We wanted to document the Government structure, our claim to sover-eignty and the unity of the Reich. This would be considered as the legal representation of the German Reich until such time as this provided the opportunity for the new order. Under no circumstances did we want to give the enemy the chance to act contrary to international law in these questions by our neglect or voluntary rejection of the role.
3. A practical idea became the guideline of all our Cabinet work: to do what-ever possible to facilitate the change from war to peace and handle the expected crisis by the best use of our labour force within the framework of what the enemy would allow.

It did not matter who took the necessary measures to ameliorate the suffer-ing of the refugees, to ease the housing shortage, improve the transport situ-ation, stimulate the economy and above all prevent famine, only that these measures should be taken as quickly and efficiently as possible. If necessary the attempt would have to be made to offer the Allies all plans, ideas, propos-als and estimates of the labour force in order to obtain the best outcome for the German people. The emergency was on such a scale that personal feel-ings, such as giving up in despair and not being prepared to take any more abuse from the enemy, had to be suppressed for the greater good. Collaboration was therefore not to be declined even if we were prisoners. The 'technical expert' Ministers who had the best understanding of matters in their own portfolios must not be allowed to stand idly by.

Following a number of conferences on 3 and 4 May, principally involving Schwerin and Speer, on the 5th a purely specialist Cabinet was formed and given the title 'Caretaker Reich-Government'. In order to emphasise its provisional character, an official form of Government and the appointment of full-blown ministers was avoided. The Cabinet had been composed bearing in mind the principles set out here earlier and with people available in the North, thus:

Head of Cabinet with portfolio of Caretaker Reich Foreign Minister and Reich Foreign Minister	Graf Schwerin von Krosigk
Chargé d'affaires, Reich Interior and Culture Ministry	Dr Stuckart
Caretaker Reich Economy and Production Ministry	Speer
Caretaker Reich Minister for Food, Farming and Forestry	Backe
Caretaker Reich Labour and Social Security Ministry	Dr Seldte
Caretaker Reich Minister for Transport and Posts	Dr Dorpmüller

Montgomery and Eisenhower were informed of this plan. The Party bosses discharged from the Government and still in the North were von Ribbentrop, Himmler, Rosenberg and the former Reich Health Minister Dr Conti. I will deal with the case of Himmler in Chapter 12. Dönitz requested Rosenberg and Dr Conti to make themselves available voluntarily to the occupying power or at least let it be known where they could be contacted. Both complied. Rosenberg had a severe sprain suffered during a drinking bout and was in the makeshift military hospital at the Flensburg-Mürwik naval college. Two days later, in a sensationalist piece of theatre, the hospital was surrounded by tanks and infantry, searched and then British troops emerged bearing the injured Rosenberg in triumph, the Nazi philosopher having 'hidden himself away there feigning injury'.

On 7 May Dönitz decided to rid himself of the former Reich Justice Minister Dr Thierach. The business of this Ministry, on which special importance was being placed in view of the reports about excesses in the concentration camps (see Chapter 12), was taken over by Secretary of State Herbert Klemm. Work in the individual portfolios was now begun according to the guidelines for the Caretaker Reich Government set out by Dönitz and Schwerin.[1]

As no national activity could take place without Allied help, the Government was limited to gathering materials, preparing reports about local situations and working out concrete plans. The results partially justified the hopes. Speer and Dorpmüller considered that it would take only six weeks to restore communications and transport to normal working. When one thinks of the communications difficulties which had been overcome almost to the end of the war despite endless air attacks, the lack of personnel, machinery and fuel: when one considers further that the surrender released innumerable technicians, vehicles of all kinds, fuel and above all specialist troops such as pioneer units, highway construction battalions and Organisation Todt units which could have been useful here, we see that the proposed deadline could have been met had the personnel and equipment not been left to rot in dumps and prison camps. The postal system would be restored in a much shorter time.

In the food sector Minister Backs and Secretary of State Riecke provided an exact picture of the situation and the future estimates to ensure equal distribution across the various zones of occupation, and identify which other measures needed to be taken to avoid catastrophe. When the Allied Control Commission and OKW met, these plans and forecasts were handed over and were apparently read with great interest. Following reports and conferences on the submissions, consent was given to continue with and update the reports.

In two cases this kind of influential reporting had an unexpected outcome. On 15 May Reich Minister Backe, and a few days later Reich Minister Dr Dorpmüller, were being flown to Allied HQ in the belief that there were to be specialist consultations. We were hopeful that they could be of use to the people in the work of rebuilding. I still see Dr Dorpmüller, old and grey, in my mind's eye as he – although very sick – took his leave of Dönitz bristling with enthusiasm. We never heard from either again, however. Much later, in captivity, we learned that they had both been arrested as soon as they touched down and placed in a prison camp. Dr Dorpmüller did not survive this change in circumstances and died in captivity. Backe, charged as a war criminal, took his own life in prison in 1949. We heard nothing more of their proposals nor of those from the other portfolio holders.

What is certain is that decisive measures for the healing of Germany and the relief of suffering in the various regions were not begun until very much later and then with little urgency. It is also certain that if the immediate post-war problems in Germany had been addressed much sooner, we would have been spared great suffering and the taxpayers and charitable organisations in the West much expense.

Chapter 12

Himmler's Dismissal

Dönitz used to round off his conferences with his officers with a free discussion. A favourite topic was the relationship of the Wehrmacht to the SS. Dönitz, opposed to the spreading or intensification of tensions because it tended to undermine confidence in the leadership and harm the fighting morale of the forces, would sidestep the question with: 'So what? Reichs-Heinrich and I are the best of friends.'

What was this friendship like in reality? In the eight months I was Dönitz's adjutant there was only a single non-official meeting between the pair of them, a dinner at FHQ in October 1944. There was no obvious good humour. On another occasion in February 1945, this time on official business, Dönitz went to see Himmler, who was also Commander-in-Chief of Army Group Vistula, at his HQ in order to discuss operational and armaments question for 1.Marine-Infanterie Division, which had been incorporated into the Army Group. These were their only meetings in the decisive six months of the war from October 1944 to April 1945. They exchanged only passing courtesies on meeting at a few situation conferences at FHQ, which both attended only irregularly. There were virtually no areas of dispute between them and each had respect for the orderly manner in which the other ran his official business, but the word 'friendship' is hardly apposite, it was much more a correct and polite relationship based on clear divisions of command. This relationship clouded over as the collapse began and led finally to separation. Later they were compelled to meet more frequently. Dönitz, as regional head, and Himmler, as Chief of Police and the *Ersatzheer*, and also possibly predestined to succeed the Führer, had both gone North. On 26 April at Schwerin they discussed the defence of the North, the maintenance of order and the refugee transports. On 27 April they met by chance at the OKW situation conference at Rheinsberg where Himmler played the Crown Prince, and on the afternoon of the 30th at the Lübeck police barracks where Himmler denied he had ever offered to capitulate as alleged by enemy radio stations on the 28th.

Especially dramatic was the meeting on the night of 30 April when Dönitz asked Himmler to come to his HQ, where he wanted to reveal his own appointment as Hitler's successor. Uncertain as to how this announcement would be received, and warned by Gauleiter Wegener, who was better informed on the political infighting, the Grossadmiral took special precautions. He reinforced the barracks guard with reliable U-boat men, and it was everything I could do to convince these enterprising submariners, sworn to loyalty to Dönitz, to exercise restraint and keep themselves as inconspicuous as possible so as not to create from the outset an atmosphere redolent with suspicion. Then I received the Reichsführer, invited his escort into the mess, and accompanied him myself to meet the new head of state. The meeting was held in private and was recorded in a memorandum by Dönitz later in these terms:

> I spoke with Himmler in my room alone. I thought it was better to place my Browning within reach on my desk underneath a sheaf of papers. I handed him the telegram to read. He went pale. He thought about it. Then he rose and congratulated me. He said, 'Let me be second man in the state'. I declined. We then had a conversation lasting about an hour in which I discussed with him my intentions and reasons for as unpolitical a government as possible if such a thing could be managed, while he insisted on the great advantages of my having him at my side. He surprised me with his belief that he had many admirers abroad. He left between 0200 and 0300 hrs knowing that I would not use him in a senior position. On the other hand I could not cut him loose completely because he controlled the police. Mind you, I knew nothing at that time of the concentration camp atrocities and murder of the Jews.

The Reichsführer left with his entourage at around 0230 hrs. The situation had been explained. Himmler came to our HQ on a few more occasions, for conferences on the occupied territories on 3 and 4 May. His position deteriorated rapidly. At 1700 hrs on 6 May Dönitz received him for the last time in order to relieve him of all his offices. The grounds for this development were as follows:

1. Dönitz considered Himmler to be political dead weight. Dönitz was convinced that while Himmler thought of himself as absolutely indispensable in the present situation, having him as a negotiating partner was out of the question. To have given him some office as a sop would also have imposed a heavy burden on Dönitz's 'Unpolitical Cabinet' and the course on which he was set.
2. In the days of the collapse, Himmler proved to be a pure fantasist. His statements were the best proof of this. He considered himself a suitable conversational partner and negotiator with Eisenhower and Montgomery. Why, these gentlemen were certainly only waiting for the chance to talk with him. As the 'factor for order in Central Europe' he and the SS were indispensable. This would bring the clash between East and West to the boil so quickly that he and the SS would tip the scales within three months. On the question of the capitulation, on 4 May he considered Norway and Bohemia as 'bargaining chips' representing valuable and cashable assets in any negotiations. In captivity, after thinking about reports from Himmler's circle I believe it is possible that his delusion about the West being prepared to negotiate with him arose not only from his fantasies but also from his own schemes for capitulation, in which he had apparently even toyed with the idea of a coup to unseat Hitler and had made some preparations along those lines.
3. In the very clear denial of 30 April at Lübeck, the Grossadmiral learned on 3 May from Himmler's own mouth that he had indeed extended peace feelers through Sweden. Dönitz was very blunt on the matter: 'Whoever lies to me once will do so often' and even stronger, 'Whoever betrays you once will do it a second time'.

Thus on 6 May Himmler disappeared from our sight, ever the optimist. 'He felt absolutely safe against discovery and would await rapid developments from concealment.' That same day, Schwerin von Krosigk told him in no uncertain terms about the probable and actual developments in the situation which would arise later, and made clear that the day could come when the leaders of the Third Reich might have to answer for what their subordinates had done, and to rebut the terrible accusations being made by enemy propaganda. This perceptive warning was ignored by Himmler not only at the expense of his subordinates and the organisation under his command, but also that of historical truth. Later Dönitz regretted releasing Himmler. Under pressure at Nuremberg, he stated that he would have arrested Himmler on the day he left had he known then about the massacres and the conditions in the concentration camps.

This raises the question: Did Dönitz really know nothing of it? The statements that have to be made here go beyond the realm of the personal. They embrace the overwhelming majority of the German people and the Wehrmacht. We know from the Nuremberg Trials, especially the statements by SS-Judge Dr Morgen, of the refined and even ingenious manner in which the true circumstances and intentions were hidden. Rumours that occasionally reached Dönitz, the source of which being mostly identified as the foreign news agencies, were disbelieved. The few concrete allegations in Germany were proved fictional. An example here was the myth of U-boat commanders Prien and Schulze being in a concentration camp. Schulze disproved the report himself when he heard it repeated by Dönitz's staff by turning up in person to argue it was not true. This of course provoked great merriment. Prien perished in the North Atlantic in March 1941 during an anti-convoy operation. False propaganda about the sea war and other theatres caused the majority of the German people to lose faith in reports emanating from foreign news agencies to which they had initially been receptive. Thus it was not the ban on listening to foreign news broadcasts that robbed the enemy news agencies of their potency but their puerile and transparent lying, which made them an easy prey for German counter-propaganda.

Obviously Dönitz knew that the inmates of concentration camps were not treated with kid gloves, while Himmler was adroit in letting the world know that he would take draconian measures against camp staff as soon as he was made aware of excesses. The court martial of two camp commandants which

Himmler instigated personally in 1944, the severe sentences and subsequent executions pacified the doubters by showing that even here an iron broom swept clean when it was necessary. In a case which Dönitz investigated in connection with the 20 July Plot, he received a satisfactory response and a quick resolution of the case.

During the capitulation, reports on concentration camp atrocities increased substantially. Generaladmiral von Friedeburg brought from Eisenhower's HQ illustrated material and newspapers with reports and photos. Some people thought they had seen a number of these pictures before at the time of Katyn. Others thought the pose of the victims and the damage to the surroundings hinted at bombing or artillery as the cause. But the remainder were very worrying. Many of the atrocities described in the reports might have been attributable to the chaotic circumstances during the collapse. The withdrawals westwards of whole camps ordered in many places, and above all the total disruption to the highways which made organised supply and the distribution of food impossible, had undoubtedly been devastating in their effects. These were things that the German people and especially millions of refugees had experienced equally.

A definite case came to light at Flensburg when a prison ship with concentration camp inmates arrived from the East. As were all vessels of the time, this steamer was overloaded and there was a food shortage aboard. The situation had become rapidly catastrophic when the ship was held up outside the port by an enemy minefield. When she finally berthed the crew and guards were found to have decamped and the harbour commander was faced with a vessel in the most appalling condition. His report was horrific. Dönitz ordered personally immediate relief supplies and medical care, which was expedited by Kapitän zur See Lüth as senior coastal station officer.

This occurrence resulted in more credence being given to enemy reports. In the knowledge that atrocities had actually been committed in this case, which were alien to the German people and Wehrmacht, it was considered a matter of honour to investigate and deal with the crime. At the suggestion of Schwerin von Krosigk, on 15 May Dönitz issued an ordinance in which the Reich Court was declared the competent authority for the investigation and prosecution of all excesses in the concentration camps. During a conference with Ambassador Murphy on another matter, Dönitz requested him to refer the ordinance to Eisenhower with the request that he enable the German authorities to exercise this function. Murphy agreed to do so, but we never received an answer.

I have no doubt whatever that such a proceeding carried out with German thoroughness, rigour and objectivity, those convicted receiving the severest punishment, would have been all the more impressive for the German people than the mixture of fact and fiction served up by press and radio. I therefore consider it regrettable both from the German and Allied points of view that the attempt by the Dönitz Government to include German judges in the prosecution of concentration camp activities was not taken up.

Above: Karl Dönitz joined the Kaiserliche Marine (Imperial Navy) as a cadet in 1910, was commissioned in 1913 and rose rapidly through the ranks. In January 1942 Hitler appointed him Commander-in-Chief of the Kriegsmarine. He succeeded Hitler as head of state after the Führer committed suicide in April 1945.

Above: Grossadmiral Dönitz (centre) with Mussolini and Hitler in 1943. In February of that year Dönitz had flown to Rome to ask the Italian dictator for the use of a number of Italian submarines as transport vessels to support German U-boat operations in Far Eastern waters, where supply was a serious problem.

Below: Dönitz at the funeral of his predecessor as Commander-in-Chief, Grossadmiral Erich Raeder, in 1960. The two men had often disagreed – significantly Raeder had opposed Dönitz's 'wolf pack' U-boat tactics.

Left: Dönitz flanked by members of his staff, directing the U-boat campaign in 1942. On the left is Kapitänleutnant Adalbert Schee, commander of *U60*, *U201* and *U2511*. On the right is Kapitän zur See Eberhard Godt, head of the U-boat Command's Operations Department.

Right: Reichsmarshall Hermann Göring, Field Marshal Wilhelm Keitel and Grossadmiral Karl Dönitz at Hitler's headquarters on 20 April 1944. Keitel also served in the Flensburg Government, and was instructed by Dönitz to sign the ratified unconditional surrender in Berlin in May 1945.

Above: Hitler shaking hands with Heinrich Himmler on the Führer's 55th birthday, on 20 April 1944, in Berlin. Keitel, Dönitz, and Field Marshal Erhard Milch are standing alongside Himmler.

Below: Walter Lüdde-Neurath (left) and Grossadmiral Dönitz leaving the Flensburg Government building (then called the Stabsgebäude) in 1945.

Above: The dramatic scene of the arrests on the morning of 23 May 1945 aboard the steamship *Patria*. From top left: the interpreter US Major General Lowell Rooks, Major General Nikolai Trusov of the Red Army, and Brigadier E. J. Foord of the British Army. From top right: Generaloberst Alfred Jodl, Grossadmiral Dönitz and Generaladmiral Hans Georg von Friedeburg, the last Commander-in-Chief of the Kriegsmarine. Representing General Eisenhower, Rooks announced the dissolution of the government and the arrest of its members. Asked if he had anything to say, Dönitz replied, 'Any words would be superfluous.' Minutes later, von Friedeburg excused himself from his personal guard and committed suicide by poison.

Right: 1000 hrs, 23 May 1945. The arrests begin. British soldiers charged into the *Patria* with machine guns and hand grenades, and ordered the government officials to put their hands up and their trousers down.

Above: A full body search was conducted on all the officials, in private, before they were paraded before the press waiting outside. According to Lüdde-Neurath, workers openly plundered the possessions of their former bosses following their arrest.

Below: Following the arrests on 23 May, Dönitz and his government were were flown to Luxembourg and installed in the Palace Hotel at Bad Mondorf, which had been converted into a prison.

Above and below: At Flensburg following the arrests: Dr. Albert Speer, Dönitz and Generaloberst Alfred Jodl face the world's press under the watch of British soldiers. Initially Speer thought that the Dönitz administration should dissolve itself following the surrender. He served as Minister of Economy and Production in the new cabinet. On his arrest, Speer said: 'Now the end has come. It is best. It was all a kind of opera beforehand.'

<u>Instrument of Surrender</u>

of

<u>All German armed forces in HOLLAND, in</u>

<u>northwest Germany including all islands,</u>

<u>and in DENMARK.</u>

1. The German Command agrees to the surrender of all German armed forces in HOLLAND, in northwest GERMANY including the FRISIAN ISLANDS and HELIGOLAND and all other islands, in SCHLESWIG-HOLSTEIN, and in DENMARK, to the C.-in-C. 21 Army Group. This to include all naval ships in these areas These forces to lay down their arms and to surrender unconditionally.

2. All hostilities on land, on sea, or in the air by German forces in the above areas to cease at 0800 hrs. British Double Summer Time on Saturday 5 May 1945.

3. The German command to carry out at once, and without argument or comment, all further orders that will be issued by the Allied Powers on any subject.

4. Disobedience of orders, or failure to comply with them, will be regarded as a breach of these surrender terms and will be dealt with by the Allied Powers in accordance with the accepted laws and usages of war.

5. This instrument of surrender is independent of, without prejudice to, and will be superseded by any general instrument of surrender imposed by or on behalf of the Allied Powers and applicable to Germany and the German armed forces as a whole.

6. This instrument of surrender is written in English and in German.

   The English version is the authentic text.

7. The decision of the Allied Powers will be final if any doubt or dispute arises as to the meaning or interpretation of the surrender terms.

B.L. Montgomery
Field-Marshal

4 May 1945
1830 hrs.

Page seven

Fotokopie der Originalurkunde nach Germany surrenders unconditionally. Facsimiles of the Documents. National Archives Publication. No. 46-4, Washington, D. C., 1945, S. 7.

Above: Partial capitulation of the German North region, Holland and Denmark is signed on May 4 1945. Field Marshal Bernard Montgomery took the unconditional military surrender from General Admiral Hans-Georg von Friedeburg. The following day, Dönitz ordered all U-boats to cease operations and return to base.

Chapter 13

Abdication?

Dönitz accepted his appointment as head of state as a commission to end the war. He believed then that Hitler, finally recognising the hopelessness of the situation, wanted to leave the way clear for capitulation by his death, something he would not have been personally prepared to do under any circumstances.

Dönitz went about his 'commission' with a heavy heart and considered it fulfilled with the signing of the instrument of total surrender early on 7 May. This act was also the last free decision of an independent German Reich Government. It had not renounced its sovereignty, but without regard to the legality of their action in international law, the victors deprived it of all possibility of effectiveness. The country was occupied. The enemy reigned.

Confronted by this situation, it seemed doubtful to Dönitz and some of his entourage that the existence of a German head of state and Government was justified or even necessary under the circumstances. During the course of 7 and 8 May this question came up in numerous conversations with members of both the Cabinet and Dönitz's staff. Corresponding to his military nature he favoured the clear and simple solution of stepping down. Speer supported him in this and did most of the urging. On the other hand, Schwerin von Krosigk called for moderation and suggested he bide his time.

The reasons for and against abdication under consideration were legion and seemed worthy of careful consideration. Thus I noted on 8 May:

Grounds for Withdrawing:

1. The commission 'to end the war' has been fulfilled.
2. Germany is totally occupied. It has neither independence at home nor representation abroad.

3. The Government is *de facto* flattened. There is no free expression of will nor possibility to govern.
4. Under these circumstances the enemy may avail himself of the expert Ministers, but give no freedom of action to the Head of Government.
5. The people are mostly indifferent to these questions. They are happy the war is over and are worried about the future from purely personal motives. We do not even know to what extent the people beyond Flensburg have knowledge of the Dönitz Government or recognise it.
6. The future fate of the Government depends on the measures the enemy takes: he can use it without recognising it. He can destroy it, he can gag it and expose it to the scorn and ridicule of public opinion throughout the world. Even within Germany, the enemy has all press, radio and propaganda organs at his disposal.
7. Personal honour and that of the Reich demand a dignified abdication.

Reasons against stepping-down were enumerated at the same time:

1. The concept of the Reich. Reich President and Government embody the unity and sovereignty of the Reich.
2. The Government must share the fate of the people.
3. To avoid famine and chaos the supra-regional direction of many questions is absolutely necessary, particularly those of food, transport, economy and finance (supply, care for those in the Russian sector, loss of aircraft). One must not cut oneself off from the chance to help the people in these matters.
4. The person of the Grossadmiral is a guarantee of stability at least during the transfer of power and the period of demobilisation. He must remain in order to reduce the danger of chaos. Moreover, as an untainted military man, Dönitz is possibly an ideal mainstay in the expected confusion of events and ideas.
5. Possibility that the enemy himself has interest in the survival of the Government: (a) as a factor for order, (b) in order to withdraw himself in the old style from immediate responsibility for coming events, and (c) political arrangement is possible if they want a strong Germany.

As a result of these discussions, having weighed up the pros and cons, the following provisional solution was decided upon: 'Stepping-down is an irrevocable decision that must therefore not be taken prematurely. The danger of being exposed to public ridicule is great, with it destruction of all idealism which speaks for staying. Abdication must ensue at the right time.'

Initially it was important to watch political developments carefully so as not to miss the right moment. As a violent solution might be imposed following Churchill's speech scheduled for 1500 hrs on 8 May, which would jeopardise any prospect of a dignified abdication, Dönitz decided to explain the situation to the German people and public. He worked on the text of this declaration with Schwerin von Krosigk and read it out live over Radio Flensburg at 1230 hrs on 8 May (Appendix 22). This was the last uncensored radio broadcast. The reaction, less to the content than the fact that Dönitz was still at liberty to speak, was immediate: the occupying Powers took over Radio Flensburg at once, thus robbing Dönitz and his Cabinet of their last public platform.

At 1630 hrs Schwerin reported on Churchill's speech. He described it as short and moderate. The British Prime Minister did not mention the Dönitz Government. This shelved the decision on whether the provisional government should stay or go. Over the next few days the general impression spread that the abdication of the Reich President, the withdrawal of the Government, or both together, would have disadvantageous consequences and be a serious error. I noted the decisive arguments in an entry on 13 May: '… Contrary to its previous attitude the enemy Press has begun to concern itself with the Dönitz Government in more or less adverse and polemic form. This fact shows that they are aware of the problem, but have not yet decided how to solve it. To solve it by stepping down voluntarily will play the enemy's game.'

It was feared that if the head of state and Government resigned it would create a vacuum in international law that might offer the Allies a sound and welcome basis for installing their own regime. The victors would then be able to claim: 'We had to take power because the German leaders ran away. We wanted a legal transfer but the German Government prevented this possibility by their flight.'

Decisive for Dönitz was the point of view first introduced into the debate by Schwerin, with which I concluded my notes: 'The Grossadmiral is the legal head of state appointed by the Führer. This legal fact is not changed by the temporary loss of sovereignty. A withdrawal by the head of state is only possible if he appoints his own successor, and if he fails to do so, the President of the Reich Court will take over.[1] In law it is not possible to extinguish the function of the head of state. This disposes of any further thinking about a voluntary resignation.'

I do not feel competent to offer an opinion on the legality of Dönitz and his Government. The work on this subject must remain the preserve of the international and constitutional lawyer. The investigation must proceed from the question of whether Hitler himself was the 'legal' head of state, or whether he made his own position unconstitutional by his first measures to reinforce his power. It is certain in any case that the 'Law Respecting the Head of State of the German Reich' of 1 August 1934 merged the offices of Reich President and Reich Chancellor in Adolf Hitler: that the German electorate gave its assent to it in the referendum of 19 August 1934 and that Hitler in consequence found general recognition as head of state both at home and abroad. It is equally certain that the same law gave Hitler the express right to nominate his Deputy. In his unopposed Reichstag declaration of 1 September 1939 at the outbreak of war with Poland he nominated Göring to succeed him, and after him Rudolf Hess. Varying this declaration by his Testament of 29 April 1945 he named Grossadmiral Dönitz as Reich President, and Goebbels as Reich Chancellor (Appendix 1 and 3).

Dönitz did not infer from his surprise appointment an absolute succession to the dictatorship unlimited by time. He emphasised frequently – and also in public – that the will of the German people alone was decisive in the question of who occupied the highest office in the land. On the other hand he inferred the right from the Testament, and from the national emergency, the duty to assume the office and act immediately. The termination of his office was *de facto* effected by his arrest (Appendix 24) but this may not have created a clear legal position. Thus the question of his forcible removal remains open for clarification as to the precise situation in international law.

Chapter 14

East or West?

It cannot be the purpose of my memoir to address problems of contemporary significance. It is also not possible to explore and exhaust all the thinking that occurred during the period of the capitulation on the East-West question. Nevertheless it is indispensable to treat the matter at this point because ultimately it is the key to the decisions taken by Dönitz at that time.

National Socialist ideology in this is known. Germany, as often previously in its history, was the defender of Western culture in the struggle against the invading hordes of Asia, while a short-sighted and unfriendly world around stabbed her in the back.

In the final weeks this mode of thought influenced Dönitz and his colleagues. The decisive point for them was the will and stance of the German people on this matter. These were known. The war against the West was never popular amongst the armed forces or the populace. They had not been educated for it. The man in the street and the soldier at the front thought of it as an unfortunate necessary evil that had been forced upon us. Only as the war went on, fed by Goebbels' propaganda, did bitterness and hate surge up from the rubble of the German cities and the graves of the innocent victims of the terror bombing. At no point did it ever approach a level sufficient to justify the many harsh measures of the occupation that followed.

In the East things were quite different. Doubts about the need for the attack on the Soviet Union were linked primarily to concerns about how the war would turn out. The clash itself was considered inevitable at some time or another by everyone. Therefore the war in the East was considered from the outset as the struggle for the destiny of the nation. It soon took a form, in my opinion not through our fault alone, which poured scorn on all international law and humanity. Mutual hate and bitterness knew no bounds, and continued unchanged to the last moment of the war.

The fundamental difference in attitude by the German people towards the enemies of East and West was seen most clearly as the Reich crumbled. Obviously on both fronts, soldiers as well as civilians made instinctive efforts to survive, but while in the spring of 1945 in East Prussia and Silesia the troops fought valiantly and desperately for every metre of German soil, in the West the will to fight on had been more or less lost after the last hopes of victory vanished at the end of 1944. After years of mental and physical over-exertion, the fighting spirit of the people turned into a spirit of resignation and then readiness to surrender. The approach of enemy forces was greeted as an end to the bombing and the other horrors of war. All they wanted now was peace.

In the East, however, a last tremendous despairing effort was made against overwhelming enemy numbers. When no success ensued, we were left with an army of millions of refugees. Here occupation did not mean freedom and peace, but dread and despair. In the West there had been signs of half-heartedness amongst troops even at Normandy, and later after the Ardennes Offensive. A falling off of operational readiness, indifference to capture and an increase in desertions was the consequence. In the East a loss of morale to anything like that extent was never seen until perhaps the very last phase. The dominating thought was not surrender, but flight. Don't fall into Russian hands! To the West! To the West! To the other side of the demarcation line!

Two cities became the symbol for the dual attitudes of people and troops. In the East there was no Paderborn, which greeted the enemy jubilantly as liberators. For them it was Breslau, where civilians and troops fought to the last with inadequate forces and weapons, devoid of any hope of relief, and only gave in when they had to on 8 May. Such a defence would have been unthinkable in the West.

When he received news of Hitler's death on 1 May, Dönitz was faced with two clear but opposing policies: 'Make peace' in the West, 'Save the people from the Russians' in the East. An overall solution was not possible because of the Allied demand for total unconditional surrender on all fronts. Consequently Dönitz decided to attempt to secure partial surrenders in the West, and to end the war in the East by pulling back the troops over the demarcation line. In which form the decision taken would proceed, and the extent to which it could be realised, are set out elsewhere in this volume. The path taken was effectively dictated by circumstances. Dönitz tried to remain unemotional and consider soberly and professionally the pros and cons of a pro-West or pro-East policy. He discussed it with Keitel, Jodl, Schwerin von Krosigk, Speer and others, even the younger officers. The intention was not to drive a wedge between the Allies, which would have endangered the peace achieved so far, and which Germany needed more than any other of the belligerents, but to find the right future direction for the German people.

After the capitulation the Government would be left powerless and forced to play the role of spectator. The prejudices felt by the great majority of the German people *against* the Russians and *for* the West as a result of tradition, education, propaganda and wartime events tended to even out in the first days of the armistice. The receptiveness for the democratic ideas of the West, and the sympathy for its representatives, cooled noticeably when the occupying authorities introduced their first measures and restrictions. The wave of hope for a far-sighted policy from the Western Allies, engendered during the collapse of the North, having its origins principally in the initial attitude of Montgomery, who had accepted the partial surrender, allowed the refugee transports and the fighting against the Soviets to continue and who advised Schörner to retreat, ebbed swiftly.

The reports from the Russian zone of occupation regarding the treatment of the civilian population sounded at first a lesser evil than had been feared. The projects for reconstruction seemed initially much more promising than in the Anglo-American zones. Thus the preconditions for an impartial overview existed.

The arguments for a re-orientation eastwards were numerous and compelling:

1. The advance of Bolshevism in Europe could no longer be halted after Germany, its strongest bulwark of resistance, had fallen. Any hesitation to realign would mean a fresh struggle and suffering for the German people and prevent reconstruction and healing of the wounds of war. It would therefore be better to take drastic measures, draw a line under the past and declare voluntarily for the Bolshevisation of Europe for the future!

2. In the case of a Third World War, which seemed inevitable sooner or later, Germany would become the battlefield and the nation would descend into civil war on an unimaginable scale. These dangers could only be avoided if the German people opted beforehand for one side or the other. This could only be the East. Independent of the final result of such a war on the European continent, the military superiority on land and the greater fighting morale of the Red Army would be decisive. To side with the Western Powers would, in the case of a military confrontation, necessarily give rise to civil war because the people in the Eastern zone could not assume an anti-Eastern stance without running the danger of being slaughtered; the Seydlitz traitor-army and German Communist Party in all four zones of occupation would also not want this.

3. Since Russia had obtained a dominant position in Central Europe that it would not be prepared to give up under any circumstances, the reunification of Germany would only be possible with Russian consent. A Bolshevist Germany might perhaps even recover the lost Eastern provinces east of the Oder-Neise Line without bloodshed: a Western-democratic Germany could never achieve this.

4. To maintain the supply of food, to the extent that it was possible to meet demand from domestic production, was only conceivable with the help of the productive agricultural regions in the East of Germany. In the West, already overpopulated even before the war, famine was bound to result.

5. The future of Germany lay principally in the East because the gigantic landmass of Russia, in many regions primitive and undeveloped, could offer German scientists, engineers and workers a quite different field of activity than the highly industrialised West. Military men, especially airmen and sailors, would have good career opportunities. The danger of the uprooting and alienation of the people of German stock was slight because thanks to their capabilities in time they would succeed in dominating the heights of the economy.

6. Finally, Bolshevism was not so 'alien' to us Germans as past propaganda had made out. By its authoritarian state structure, the progressive ideas of Socialism and in many other areas it resembled Hitler's Germany very closely.

These arguments for political change and a new direction for German public opinion found fertile soil in the deep disappointment and oppressive despair of those days. The developments in the Western zone did much to reinforce the prospects. Over-population, the distress of the refugees, housing short-ages, social misery and high unemployment, and a grim situation as regards food supply would, so it was believed, cause a radicalisation of the masses to favour the fruits of Bolshevism. The apparent total inability of the Anglo-Americans to understand this, the attitude of their occupation troops and the first measures of the military governors in the Western zones, seemed to encourage the development of pro-Russian sentiments and stand the initial sympathies for the West on their heads.

We had the impression that the Russians were determined not to let slip the chances which presented themselves to win over the Germans. Stalin's utterance 'Germany must not be dismembered', a clever, much more astute form of propaganda for the German mentality in press and radio, rumours of the emphatic reserve and correctness of individual Russian garrisons and the apparent equality in personal relations all went to confirm this impression. In the first weeks after the capitulation in the North, such thinking and opinions were very prevalent. The attitude of many soldiers and junior officers underwent an abrupt change. Ideas that we had surrendered to the wrong side and that the Baltic fleet should have run into Königsberg or Kronstadt instead of Kiel, Flensburg and Copenhagen, were voiced loudly. It was even suggested that it was not too late to change and make the leap to the East overnight. That this was possible a commander proved a few days after the capitulation by sailing unnoticed along the coast of Mecklenburg, going ashore in a rubber dinghy, visiting his family and returning to Flensburg the way he had come next evening.

Dönitz followed these developments with great concern. He had no sympathy whatever for the pro-Russian argument. The dangers seemed worse for him, as also for the Cabinet members, some of whom had connections to the Eastern neighbour. The freedom of the individual and the inviolability of law were two basic conditions of national life without which Germany could not exist in the long run. These seemed secure only in the democratic West. Above all he held the racial survival of Germanism under apparently friendly Russian leadership to be an illusion. 'Who will guarantee the existence of the German people 100 years from now?' he asked. Whole layers of population would be destroyed or transplanted through planned subversion, miscegenation and international proletarian policy. The term 'German' would eventually not apply to anyone. Thus he decided against the 'Asiatic East' and in favour of the 'Christian West'.

Dönitz expressed these ideas generally to the British and American heads of the Control Commission before the meeting with the Russian generals in his office at Flensburg-Mürwik. For the same reason on the afternoon of 17 May he also received – as an exception to his general rule – the British journalist Mr Ward, his hope being perhaps to create better understanding of the situation and developments in Germany. Although his listeners seemed impressed, these attempts had no lasting success, as the first two years of Western occupation policy have shown. All the same, his attitude had an immediate effect: his clear approach, his influence on and alignment of the officer corps,[1] still directed from the top downwards and maintaining its discipline, prevented politically unpleasant consequences arising from the violent mood-swings of the time.

Chapter 15

The Allied Control Commission

Shortly after the unconditional surrender came into effect, the 'Allied Control Commission at OKW' arrived at Flensburg. Its official task was to oversee the correct observance of the capitulation conditions by the OKW and give instructions as to the demobilisation of the German forces. The Commission consisted initially only of a mixed Anglo-American Staff under Major-General Rooks (USA) and Brigadier Foord (Great Britain). The staff had amongst its numbers many purely military advisors and a huge team of technical specialists whose interest was the military administration. There was a great deal of activity between them and the 'Caretaker Reich Government'. This seemed to provide the hoped-for opportunities to influence developments in Germany along the guidelines mentioned in Chapter 11. The memoranda and practical proposals were received with interest, which expressed itself in numerous discussions aboard the *Patria*. On the Allied side, emphasis was laid on the problems of food supplies and road communications. These meetings were cool but correct. The definite distancing of the British was met by equal reserve by ourselves, all attempts at fraternisation being doomed to failure. On two visits by Dönitz to Rooks, the usual custom of paying shipboard honours – piping the side, presenting arms and reception by the officers – was maintained, and the Control Commission even respected the enclave, in which until a short time before our arrest 'Guard Batallion *Dönitz*' remained under arms under the command of Korvettenkapitän Kremer, and it was respected as sovereign territory.

Before his arrest, Dönitz met with the head of the Control Commission three times. The first time he was 'requested' by telephone to come to the *Patria* at midday on 13 May. Though the form of the summons was thought discourteous, the meeting was not. Rooks had an order for the arrest of

Generalfeldmarschall Keitel and expressed his regrets. Dönitz took the opportunity to mention the urgent problem of restoring order in Germany. Keitel was notified of his arrest half an hour later. It was done correctly. He was given the opportunity to take his leave of Dönitz and sufficient time to prepare for the flight, on which he was expressly allowed to be accompanied by his adjutant and valet. Upon leaving he voiced his suspicion that this premature and singular arrest had to do with the shooting of fifty British and Empire PoWs after the 'Great Escape' at Stalag Luft III in 1944. He had attempted to dissuade Hitler from it but considered himself covered by Hitler's express order. Generaloberst Jodl took over from Keitel as Head of the OKW.

The second summons for Dönitz was a more easy-going affair in which he was questioned by Rooks and Mr Murphy, Eisenhower's political advisor, on his claim to be the legitimate head of state. Murphy avoided making any comment on what Dönitz said, as was to be expected, and went over copies of the signals appointing him, which Dönitz had previously assembled as evidence.

The third meeting took place on 20 May in his office, where he had invited the two heads of the Control Commission. As we were not sure how this invitation would be received, I was given the job of finding out whether it would be accepted. I was told it would be provided it was presented 'in due form'. We succeeded in it correctly. In a talk lasting an hour or so, Dönitz spoke mainly on the situation in the interior and the measures he thought necessary to restore normal civilian life. For this purpose he provided a memorandum about the Caretaker Reich Government. He also discussed the basic East-West question and the dangers that would result from the break-up of Germany. The two generals were visibly impressed.

For the duration of this conference, Dönitz had had a bust of the Führer removed, which had been left in the office of the base commander that he now occupied. This was in accord with an instruction he had issued that everything possible had to be avoided which the victors might interpret as provocative and might hamper co-operation. The reintroduction of the traditional military salute in the Wehrmacht in place of the obligatory Hitler-salute, and the removal of portraits of the Führer and other Party bosses from the rooms to which the Allies had access were also part of this policy.

Dönitz was not prepared to make wider concessions, however. He would not order the removal of Nazi insignia as advised by a number of senior officers since they formed part of the uniform in which a man had fought for six years. Similarly he refused to order the concealment or defacing of awards and decorations. These came under the protection of internationally agreed conventions and Dönitz considered it dishonourable to deny or deface in defeat the honours that a man had received and worn in wartime. The Army wanted to make suggestions here. The target of their attack was the German Cross in Gold, which – although awarded for military valour – was jokingly referred to as 'the super-big Party Badge' even during the war, and probably for this reason was a keenly sought-after 'souvenir' for soldiers of the victor states. It was also suggested that the swastika on the Iron Cross should be filed off, and in many cases the holders did this themselves either because they wanted to distance themselves from the regime or hoped to retain the medal. This latter was a false hope: contrary to international law and the conventions signed by Britain, France and the USA, the wearing of such decorations was forbidden and in many cases they were forcibly confiscated.

On the question of the national war flag, Dönitz left the initiative to the enemy and refused to issue the instruction himself. Thus the war flag on the flagpole before the Government HQ at Flensburg was not hauled down until the Allies expressly ordered it at midday on 10 May. This was in parallel with an order that the hoisting of the swastika flag was generally forbidden. Moreover, Dönitz gave the Wehrmacht an instruction that 'defamatory' orders were to be refused and left to the enemy to carry out himself. Thus he convinced German forces in Norway not to obey the orders of the British occupiers given to the Wehrmacht HQs to arrest SS and Party men themselves, since this was in conflict with the conditions of the surrender and the honour of the Wehrmacht.

On the evening of 17 May the Russian Staff under Major-General Truskov attached to the Control Commission arrived at Flensburg. Because different approaches to the three Allies could have worked to our disadvantage, the Russians were supplied with the same material on military and economic questions (e.g. strengths and disposition of all German fighting forces at the war's end and on certain other key dates) and were also given the same proposals we had worked on. It was noticeable but understandable that the Russians were more interested in what was going on in the Western zones than in their own, something it was clear the Anglo-Americans did not like.

In contrast to their Western colleagues the Russians treated their German counterparts with exquisite courtesy. This behaviour was very different to the official Russian attitude in the press and on the radio, however. Although they had taken a back seat in the capitulation negotiations, in a report they demanded that the German Government remove itself to Berlin 'where it belongs by rights' and gradually Russian propaganda built up its attacks and invective culminating in a demand for our immediate 'liquidation'. For this reason, and from other indications, we began to expect our arrest daily with effect from 19 May.

Chapter 16

The Arrest of the Caretaker Reich Government

I contemplated for a while whether the full account of the arrest of the Government and OKW at Flensburg was useful or even necessary. I decided against it for an initial press interview, but the reaction to the omission surprised me. Not only was I suspected of concealing it deliberately, but I also came across descriptions of our capture, which did not match the facts or gave details of this very unpleasant event in a distorted or exaggerated form. I now accept that remaining silent on grievous moments in relationships between peoples or persons is seldom crowned with lasting success, and risks creating the opposite effect to that desired. Therefore I consider a clear and sober account of the events to be justified, not only to complete the story, but to rebut exaggerated and mischievous rumours.

Twice in the course of the last weeks of the war Dönitz ran the risk of capture during the fighting. The first was on the night of 19 April when prior warning of the collapse on the Oder front from the Army General Staff did not reach us and Dönitz only left *Koralle* a few hours before the arrival of the Russians thanks to his own premonition. The second occurred during the rapid advance of British forces to Lübeck on 2 May. He avoided this by immediately transferring his HQ from Plön to Flensburg.

This new HQ was within the territory surrendered to Montgomery with effect from 0800 hrs on 5 May, and Dönitz was liable to arrest at any time. In the negotiations we had been granted an extraterritorial zone or 'enclave' to allow the Government and OKW to function, but Montgomery had not included it in the instrument of surrender because he did not have the authority. Although to my knowledge the decision was never confirmed to us officially, the British respected a small area at Flensburg-Mürwik after their occupation and the exact boundaries were agreed between Jodl and the local British commander.

The Government and OKW remained here unsupervised and unmolested. Officers and the guard battalion retained their weapons, and after the unconditional surrender came into effect on 9 May nothing changed immediately. This tacit recognition of authority gave neither Dönitz not the Control Commission any false expectations regarding the duration of this provisional situation, and neither did Dönitz share the illusions of some of his colleagues that in accordance with international practice the victors would respect the integrity of the head of state as they had done previously and would do so later in the case of Japan. Personally, he was convinced that he would remain unmolested only so long as the enemy needed him for the smooth execution of the capitulation.

The Allies had apparently not come to a decision how they should treat the head of state and his Government in the first days of its establishment, nor as to the time and manner of ending it. Murphy's visit seems to have influenced the manner, and the arrival of the Russian Staff at the Control Commission on the evening of 17 May the time. The investigation into the question of 'legality' by Murphy, and his show of scepticism when Dönitz could produce no written document except the telegrams, led to the assumption that at least for the purpose of arrest the legality of Dönitz and his Cabinet would be challenged, or cast into grave doubt, in order to avoid the eventual claims in constitutional and international law and custom. Shortly afterwards we were confirmed in this suspicion when the press began denying the legality of Dönitz and called him 'the self-proclaimed successor'.[1]

On the afternoon of 22 May when I told Dönitz that I had received a telephoned order from Rooks' Staff on the Major-General's behalf that he was to present himself with Jodl and von Friedeburg at 0945 hrs next morning aboard the *Patria*, after a short silence he said, 'Pack your bags'. The day of our arrest was imminent, and it played out like this:

Punctually at the ordered time we arrived at the *Patria*. The first glance confirmed our assumption that we were prisoners of war: no reception at the gangway, no officer of the watch to receive us, no honour guard presenting arms. Instead only a motley crew of press reporters. We got the impression that some of them would stop at nothing to get a good photo or story, as one might expect in such a situation. In the ship's bar, now fitted out as a conference room, we waited five minutes before Major-General Rooks entered followed by Brigadier Foord, Major-General Truskov and the interpreters. The Allied officers sat along one side of the table facing Jodl, Dönitz and von Friedeburg on the other. Rooks as spokesman made a short introductory speech and then stated that he had received orders from Allied HQ to arrest the Government and OKW (Appendix 24). The German officers assembled had therefore to consider themselves 'prisoners of war'. He concluded with a few observations about our future treatment: 'Luggage, as much as you need, departure 1330 hrs. From now on an Allied officer will always accompany you.' In response to Major-General Rooks' closing question if the Grossadmiral wished to say anything, Dönitz said that in this situation any reply would be superfluous, and he wished to leave with the other officers.

As we were getting into our car I looked around for the officer appointed as our escort but could not see him. Dönitz, neither used to waiting nor willing to do so, told the driver to drive off. Just then I saw an American naval officer go running to another car, which then sped after us. Dönitz, who appeared amused, told our driver to slow down 'to spare the poor fellow any unpleasantness'. Up to this point everything had been done by the book. We saw no reason to think that our treatment would change, but von Friedeburg thought differently. After we left the *Patria* he exchanged a few words with Dönitz. He was seriously considering whether he could go along with 'the circus that is now beginning with all its attendant humiliations'. Dönitz believed that we would be treated according to the terms of the Geneva Convention, an illusion that was very soon shattered. Immediately after this talk von Friedeburg found his worst apprehensions confirmed when in front of the Government HQ he witnessed one of the most disgraceful scenes of the day and shortly after took his own life by poison. Undoubtedly he was appalled by what went on, but may already have decided beforehand on his course of action. As a soldier he had done his duty as negotiator and envoy to the, for him, especially bitter end, and I cannot condemn him sparing himself the dishonour of being put on trial as a criminal.

We had just begun making the last arrangements for our departure when at 1100 hrs a British Army captain and some soldiers appeared and with a lack of any military decorum or human decency ordered Dönitz to 'get on with it'. In vain I attempted to reason with him that his orders 'We're leaving at once' and 'only one suitcase' were contrary to the instructions we had received from Major-General Rooks. Because it would have taken time to repack our things into one suitcase each, he made an exception for Dönitz and me and we were allowed to take two. By the time the Allied press had finished with this incident we had eight suitcases each and it was revealed that we wore silk underwear.

The British officer ignored my polite request to show some respect because the house was in mourning (Kapitän zur See Lüth had been accidentally shot dead by a sentry a few days before). On the contrary he sauntered through the house in a jocular manner, and Frau Lüth fled in tears with her husband's decorations. As I was at a loss what to do in such a situation, I requested our US officer escort, who was clearly not happy with the conduct of the British captain, to look after the decorations, to which he agreed.

We were now driven under heavy guard to Police HQ at Flensburg. Here we were subjected to so intimate a body search that words fail me to describe it. Suffice to say that nothing remained unexamined. In view of this experience, which was repeated on a somewhat reduced scale upon our arrival at Bad Mondorf prison in Luxembourg, I consider it unlikely that Göring himself could have smuggled through the poison that enabled him to cheat the hangman in his last hour. Our luggage was searched in our absence, and besides the removal of papers considered useful by the Allies for official purposes, a number of private items such as maps, fountain pens, photographs and so forth were confiscated. Dönitz's field-marshal's baton, his interim baton, and rank insignia such as shoulder straps were also taken. In view of the value of the two batons I doubt that they went via official channels. It would have been easy to have put these things beyond the victors' reach during the preceding fourteen days, but since their seizure would be contrary to the Geneva Convention we had not thought of doing so, and we assumed that the enemy would abstain on the grounds of military honour (Appendix 25).

After a ninety-minute wait in the hall of the building, Reich Minister Schwerin von Krosigk and the members of the Caretaker Reich Government, and also Jodl with the OKW chiefs, were brought up under heavy guard. They reported on their treatment in the HQ building. The enclave had been surrounded by a huge force of tanks, infantry and military police to crush any resistance by the Germans. This was purely for effect, theatre, the impression of a dangerous military operation carried out with aplomb. These soldiers of the British 11th Armoured Division were good actors. The 11th had earned respect from the German Wehrmacht and we recognised the buffalo on the upper arm as the insignia of a brave and honourable unit. The British commandant of Flensburg, Brigadier Churcher, was in charge of the fiasco. He had previously acted unobjectionably in his dealings with us and so we assumed that the script had been written at a higher level. The only shame attaching to the 11th Armoured Division was its participation in the events of 23 May 1945.

This is what went on. Every day at 1000 hrs Schwerin von Krosigk had assembled the Caretaker Reich Cabinet for a short conference at which some senior officers would also take part. Shortly after the session began British soldiers burst into the room with machine-pistols and hand-grenades at the ready. 'Hands up!' 'Trousers down!' Then followed the full body search, which we at least had been allowed to endure in private. Apparently this happened in the presence of female secretaries, an allegation I can well believe having seen the photos in some Allied newspapers running a caption that 'the Herrenvolk were surprised in bed'.

Next, the occupants at HQ were herded into the forecourt and forced to spend a long period with hands on head for the benefit of Press photographers, subjected to insults by the British soldiery and the curious stares of local citizens. After much going back and forth the officers were then permitted to fetch their luggage under guard from rooms that had been thoroughly ransacked. The thieves did not even have the decency to hide from the eyes of their former owners the watches, radios and other items of value they had looted. At police HQ there was another 'search' of bodies and luggage. Jodl called it 'organised plunder' and I could not argue with him.

Finally von Friedeburg's adjutant was brought in. After his principal charge had committed suicide, his American officer looked round vainly for a substitute. Since there was no successor to the 'C-in-C Kriegsmarine', and on the sound military basis that any choice was better them none, he attached himself to this adjutant, active until 1 May 1945 with the U-boat arm. The adjutant was thus forced to deputise for his deceased principal at all stages of the future proceedings and even occupied what would have been von Friedeburg's cell at Nuremberg. Von Friedeburg himself did not escape the 'dishonourable treatment' he feared by committing suicide. His body was looted, an act for which the British issued an apology later, to my knowledge the only time they ever did such a thing. Late that afternoon we were loaded into lorries and driven to the airfield guarded by a squadron of tanks. From there we were flown to Luxembourg and installed in the Palace Hotel at Bad Mondorf, which had been successfully converted into a prison.

The Dönitz Government in Modern Academic Research

Walter Baum

Dedicated to Percy Ernst Schramm on the
seventieth anniversary of his birth

Chapter 1

The Struggle for the Succession

As Speer describes, the in-fighting behind the scenes to succeed Hitler commenced early on.[1] Up to 1943 Reichsmarschall Göring had no challenger. Within the Party ranks he had been deemed the 'Crown Prince' as early as the late autumn of 1934[2] and he was declared the immediate successor publicly in Hitler's Reichstag speech of 1 September 1939 with Hess in second place.[3] After Hess' flight to Britain on 10 May 1941, Hitler issued an edict on 29 June 1941 confirming Göring as 'the only successor'.[4] With the gradual eclipse of the Luftwaffe, perceived clearly once the major planned night air raids by Allied bombers on German cities began from the spring of 1943, his star sank so rapidly[5] that the existing arrangement for the succession was no longer so certain.

By virtue of his office as head of the Reich Chancellery, the question concerned Hans Lammers particularly. In the autumn of 1943 he therefore commissioned Percy Schramm, Professor of Modern History at Göttingen, to prepare examples from history as proposals for an electoral college[6] which would put into concrete form Hitler's vague ideas of a 'Führer-election' after Göring had passed on.[7] After several weeks' study, Schramm submitted a memorandum recommending a conclave with a secret ballot along the lines by which the Pope and the Doge of Venice were elected. The idea behind this recommendation was to suppress the influence of the Party and obstruct the possibility of Himmler's succession. The memorandum was merely an academic exercise, for Lammers dared not show it to Hitler, and it disappeared into a safe.

Although growing cooler towards Göring as time went on,[8] Hitler was not prepared to cut him adrift, the main reason for this being his dislike of having new faces in his entourage.[9] He had a certain predilection for the old SA street-fighters[10] – provided they represented no challenge to him – and not least reasons of prestige[11] also played their part in ensuring that all efforts to set Göring aside, or bring him to account, were doomed to fail.[12] In January 1945 when Lammers confided to Bormann his concerns about the succession, he was told: 'If the question were not already settled, I believe that the Führer would not nominate the Reichsmarschall today. However, I doubt that he will change the nomination he has already made.'[13]

Hitler himself considered the matter unsatisfactory and reportedly racked his brains for a solution, though without success.[14] Thus on 22 April 1945, despite the objections of his generals, he confirmed his choice of Göring as his successor to lead the necessary negotiations with the enemy when the time came.[15] Thus the Reichsmarschall was designated chief negotiator. Despite his outward confidence,[16] inwardly Göring did not feel secure of his position. The cool leave-taking between himself and the Führer on 21 April would have reinforced his doubts:[17] when he received the report of Hitler's decision to remain in Berlin, he was probably lured by the idea of power but hesitated.[18] He suspected that his 'arch-enemy' Bormann was plotting against him: 'He is just waiting to bump me off. If I act now, I shall be branded a traitor: if I do not act, they will say that in the most difficult time I failed.' Even when Lammers, who had been at Berchtesgaden, rushed to Obersalzberg to confirm unequivocally the legality of the succession arrangement, Göring was unhappy about proceeding independently, and accepted instead the suggestion of General Koller, Chief of the Luftwaffe General Staff, to send a telex to the Reich Chancellery with a time limit for reply.

This set off the avalanche. The text of the message was so long and pompous that it required abridgement and modification for rapid transmission.[19] What remained was neither an ultimatum nor evidence of high treason, especially since Göring ended by hoping that Hitler would be able – note well, 'with God's help' – to get away from Berlin.[20] Moreover, at the same time he sent signals to Bormann and the Luftwaffe adjutant at FHQ, Oberst von Below, with a request to persuade Hitler to leave the Reich capital. Bormann probably presented Hitler with an edited version – a kind of 'Ems despatch' – and stopped von Below from complying with Göring's request.[21] Thus he managed to have the Reichsmarschall branded a 'traitor'.

At first Hitler took no steps against the old 'paladin' except to forbid him to act independently. During the course of the evening when he heard reports about Göring's alleged negotiations with foreign representatives, however, he saw in it a connection to the earlier telex, i.e. treason against both the state and Hitler's person as leader. Whereas he had tolerated the telex,[22] now he reacted more fiercely.[23] Cloaked with his morbid distrust,[24] fortified by the atmosphere of impending doom of the time, which Bormann had done everything he could to deepen, he relieved the Reichsmarschall of all his offices and decorations. He did not seek an explanation nor set up an enquiry. Bormann was told to send Göring a telex drawing attention to the capital nature of his sins and required the 'voluntary' laying down of all his offices should he wish to avoid 'other steps' being taken.[25] Publicly the disinheritance was glossed over with the story of a 'long-standing heart condition' which had now entered 'an acute phase': the Reichsmarschall had therefore 'at this time requested to be relieved of his offices and responsibilities which demand the employment of all his strength'.[26] Whether and to what extent the general public was deceived by this – if they learned of it – is difficult to say: for all those in the know, or reflective thinkers, it was the admission, all too late, that Göring had finally shot his bolt. He yielded quickly,[27] and especially since he continued to recognise Hitler as Führer,[28] the latter did not consider it necessary to follow up the threats with action.

The precipitate arrest of the Reichsmarschall by the Obersalzberg SS detachment seems to have been ordered independently by Bormann in anticipation of the Führer's order.[29] The term 'Ehrenhaft' – arrest without loss of honour – was a calculated cover to protect his own back in the event that things turned sour unexpectedly.[30] The SD chief Kaltenbrunner had not been informed of the operation nor initially had he been told anything about the Göring affair. He heard of it during a trip to Austria, which he broke off immediately to take charge of things personally at Berchtesgaden.[31] By then the situation had changed, Hitler's naval adjutant Konteradmiral von Puttkamer having lifted the SS cordons with his own entourage and restored some order. Puttkamer had no high opinion of Göring but on this occasion was not convinced of his guilt and was averse to having Party intrigues add to the chaos surrounding the collapsing Reich. Kaltenbrunner endorsed the

Admiral's actions since he shared his doubts about the accusation but acted against the Reichsmarschall's Staff in hindsight.[32] Only the energetic intervention of Koller, Chief of the Luftwaffe General Staff, and the existence of discord between the local SD and SS, who in the confusion remained at odds[33] saved the officers.[34]

By this time, Hitler had ended his life in Berlin after expelling Göring from the Party in the text of his Political Testament, and had established the new succession.[35] Bormann therefore decided to concentrate on persecuting the Reichsmarschall and threatened his own people on the Obersalzberg with death or 'Sippenhaft'[††36] if they failed to liquidate 'the traitors' should Berlin fall. In the confusion of the collapse the order was ignored. It does not seem very likely that Bormann wanted to help Dönitz rid himself of the other candidates:[37] it is more probable that he hoped to drag Göring down into the abyss with him out of personal hatred.[38]

Despite being disinherited, Göring still thought himself the rightful successor to Hitler.[39] Probably the worst reports only reached him through normal channels – the OKW Command Staff South[40] – but there could be no doubt about the message they bore. Because he thought that the whole proceeding against him resulted from Hitler's error and the intrigues of Bormann, Göring considered it null and void.[41] Moreover, he still prided himself on being the most suitable negotiator with the Western Allies[42] but was unaware that the time when they might have accepted him in the role[43] was long past.[44] He was surprised to discover that they thought of him as a 'war criminal'.[45] Even at Mondorf Camp where he joined the other prominent prisoners, he believed he ranked as 'First Man' until the unmistakable rejection of him by the others convinced him to the contrary.[46]

By the same measure that Göring's star waned, Himmler's rose. Since July 1944 at the latest, according to Hitler he had been *de facto* the most powerful man in the state.[47] In government circles he was considered to be the leading candidate for the succession, from which though basically an underling he derived further encouragement.[48] Possibly Hitler toyed with the idea of nom-

---

†† The detention of the families of persons suspected of anti-state activities.

inating the Reichsführer-SS, but internal opposition from the Party and his own antipathy towards 'non-musical' people would have turned him against the idea.[49] Despite the humiliations on the Upper Rhine[50] and with Army Group Weichsel[51] Himmler had not been sufficiently damaged[52] for him to feel that he was disqualified as 'heir to the throne' after Göring had been eclipsed.[53] It was for that reason that he demonstrated his claim to be the leading candidate by sitting in Hitler's chair in his absence during the situation conference at OKW HQ on 27 April 1945.[54] He equalled Göring in the fantasies of his own importance,[55] but from the Allied point of view the atrocities of the SS made him far less attractive than the Reichsmarschall. It can be assumed that the Wehrmacht recognised him as a candidate but the majority were opposed. In the case of the 'official' nomination by Hitler the 'legitimacy' of the appointment might have held sway[56] and the fear of civil war at the moment of collapse might have silenced the doubters. Dönitz had been ready to subordinate himself to Himmler[57] until Hitler struck the latter from the reckoning, as he had done with his former helper and current rival Göring, for their respective efforts to negotiate with the West through Sweden.[58]

As the result of foreign radio reports that the Reichsführer-SS had prepared the ground for surrender talks,[59] on 29 April 1945 Bormann requested Dönitz in the name of the Führer to act 'lightning fast and steely hard' against the new traitor.[60] Dönitz vacillated: he agreed to meet Himmler at the Lübeck police barracks, where the latter denied any contact with the enemy and swore loyalty.[61] Dönitz believed him and for him that ended the matter. Even if Himmler had admitted the true facts, the Admiral would still have sought an amicable agreement.[62] Whether such restraint would have been right or necessary is a question open to debate.[63] A clash between Himmler and Dönitz was not to be avoided, however.

How and why Hitler decided in favour of Dönitz as his successor can only be guessed at. It was certainly not to spare the Party the odium of the surrender and put all the blame on the fighting forces, for he had too much respect for Dönitz for that.[64] After a major disagreement soon after Dönitz was appointed Kriegsmarine Commander-in-Chief, the relationship between the two had improved from not merely correct but trusting. Much more so than Raeder, Dönitz had sought a good personal rapport with the Führer from the outset and had succeeded in his aim.[65]

Hitler began to 'draw him closer', openly preferred him and did not lose faith in him when the U-boat War folded.[66] Dönitz knew how to keep hope alive for a successful revival of U-boat activity[67] and maintain unbroken the will of the Kriegsmarine to fight.[68] Either he believed in it or acted as if he did in order that Hitler should not feel 'betrayed'.[69] He expected to see the ruthless prosecution of the war ordered in the Political Testament.[70] On his own admission he was surprised by his appointment,[71] although for some time beforehand people in Hitler's close circle considered it an almost established fact,[72] and even his adjutant had heard talk of this kind.[73]

Due to the impending collapse and the confused circumstances in Berlin it was not considered likely that another instruction setting out the 'succession to the throne' would be forthcoming[74] after Hitler had not taken the opportunity previously when the circumstances were more favourable.[75] Dönitz was intending to surrender the troops under his command after Hitler fell in Berlin, then die in battle. In the late afternoon of 30 April, however, he received the first of Bormann's three signals in which he was informed of his appointment to succeed Hitler in place of Göring.[76]

Because there was no mention of the Führer's death in the first signal, although Hitler had taken his own life hours before, Dönitz decided he must be still alive and replied immediately with a declaration of loyalty.[77] He promised to make further efforts to extract Hitler from Berlin although he would accept his appointment should 'Fate compel me'. The ambiguous structure of the declaration that he would 'fight this war to its conclusion in the manner which the heroic struggle of the German people demands'[78] could easily be interpreted in Berlin in the light of his previous attitude as an undertaking to fight on ruthlessly, but was in reality a negative promise. Naval officers at SKL who feared Dönitz would 'carry on regardless'[79] knew nothing of the change which had come over him lately.

Although by his written dispositions Hitler had settled the matter of the succession beyond question, Bormann appears to have pursued his own political agenda. As executor of the Last Testament and the new Party Minister, apparently he wanted to secure for himself the maximum influence with the new head of state. In order to make himself indispensable from the outset, he fed Dönitz the signals respecting his appointment in such a way that Dönitz remained unaware of the 'current situation', i.e. that Hitler was dead. Independent, clear-cut decisions could not be taken if Hitler was still in charge. Meanwhile negotiations were proceeding with the Soviets in Berlin, something from which Bormann expected much.[80] For this reason he postponed going to Dönitz, and the Russians knew of Hitler's death before Dönitz did. When the talks came to nothing and Bormann was ready to break out from Berlin, he requested ahead that the Testament should not be made public until he arrived, i.e. he could still see some advantage in holding all details in reserve. Only in the third signal did he reveal the written succession with full permission to make it known.

In all probability Bormann met his death in the early hours of 2 May 1945 in Berlin's Ziegelstrasse.[81] Meanwhile Dönitz had acted on the advice of Schwerin von Krosigk and given orders for the arrest of Bormann and Goebbels should they surface in his HQ.[82] This was not the beginning of a major cleansing operation because Dönitz did not know the overall criminal nature of the regime,[83] and at most had knowledge of individual excesses and atrocities by the 'Nazi elite'.[84] Thus his Government was not sufficiently separate from the previous one,[85] and its period of existence was rather 'the last days of the Third Reich' than the first days of a new regime.

Chapter 2

Making the Dönitz Government

Although Dönitz was Hitler's right-hand man, the Führer did not bequeath him all his powers as he had promised to do for Göring and Hess, but limited him to the offices as head of state (Reichspräsident), Minister for War and Kriegsmarine commander-in-chief.[1] Even though Dönitz had been a convinced National Socialist, apparently Hitler did not think he possessed his own comprehensive 'Führer-qualities'.[2] He had therefore made Goebbels Reich Chancellor, Schörner Army Commander-in-Chief and Bormann the new Party leader with the rank and title of a Reich Minister. Furthermore he wrote to Dönitz and the other Ministers about prosecuting the war 'with all available means', assuring them that his 'spirit would remain amongst them' and that his racial ideology had to 'scrupulously' observed. Even total catastrophe could not extract from the mania some vestige of reason and decency.

Dönitz did not see the whole Testament until the winter of 1945[3] but the third signal from Berlin had given him incisive instructions of a personal nature to create a successor government.[4] During consultations with his closest colleagues,[5] Schwerin von Krosigk pointed out that the head of a totalitarian regime should not allowed himself to be so hog-tied by his predecessor,[6] and Dönitz therefore reverted to the powers of plenipotentiary conveyed in the first signal '… especially if the last instructions cannot be realised, as a result of the development of the situation'.[7]

He put off appointing a Cabinet,[8] since all that mattered to him at this juncture was to bring the war to a speedy end and find a Foreign Minister able to negotiate with the enemy. Neurath had a certain credibility in foreign affairs and the necessary experience but could not be contacted. The narrow-minded Ribbentrop considered himself the only man for the job[9] but was never in the running. Thus Dönitz offered the job to former Finance Minister

Graf Schwerin von Krosigk who had made an impression on him and whose opinions expressed in conferences over the last few days coincided with his own.[10] For a brief while Schwerin wavered: he felt he would be merely a stop-gap, but his proposal that a prominent industrialist or businessman such as Vögler, Bücher, Lindemann or Münchmeyer should be appointed fell on deaf ears.[11] These names would be 'programmed' to show that the idea of power politics was dead, and the future intent was to pursue economic ends. Dönitz wanted to lose no time, however, and Schwerin took on a job 'which would earn him no laurels'.[12]

In order to shed some of the burden and distance himself as head of state from the Wehrmacht, on 1 May Dönitz promoted his trusted colleague von Friedeburg, Commanding Admiral U-boats, to Generaladmiral and Kriegsmarine Commander-in-Chief.[13] He also wanted a change of OKW leadership.[14] Keitel had been away from the front for years and when he had been there was little admired.[15] His association with a string of Hitler's criminal orders also made him too heavily contaminated for the new 'Government'. Dönitz and his new Foreign Minister agreed on Generalfeldmarschall Manstein as the best successor as OKW chief, but the approach to him encountered a number of uncertainties and misunderstandings, and failed.[16] Later, Dönitz was urged several times by one of his old colleagues to cut Keitel adrift,[17] but while he was thinking about it the Allies relieved him of the decision by announcing the arrest of Keitel as a prisoner of war on 13 May 1945.[18] The outcome was that on Dönitz order, and with Eisenhower's approval, Jodl took over the position of chief of the OKW and held that office until the end of the 'Government'.[19]

The location of the HQ and seat of Government was particularly discussed at OKW. For a short while opinions had been divided between Prague (Keitel) and Berchtesgaden (Jodl).[20] Both venues were situated within a relatively large and enclosed German power base. Since any transfer from Schleswig-Holstein could only proceed by air, however, and the Germans no longer controlled the air over their territory, from these outset the plans had no prospect of adoption. Moreover, Bohemia was becoming daily less secure, and insurrection was expected at any moment. After an 'enclave' at Flensburg-Mürwik had been negotiated with the British 21st Army Group[21] the debate ended and Flensburg became the seat of government. No occupation troops were sent in, and German officers retained their weapons after 9 May. Even a guard battalion was approved.[22] Links to subordinates and the outside world were severed, however. If in the first days of May 1945 the Government – theoretically at least – was able to reach sections of the population through Radio Flensburg, and Schwerin von Krosigk had even managed to send some telexes to German missions abroad, these facilities were blocked on 8 May.[23] Applications to re-open the radio stations were apparently 'taken into consideration', but nothing came of them.[24]

That only 'freedom on a dog-leash' was being enjoyed was not always perceived by everyone.[25] The victors had not abandoned their programme to root out National Socialism and militarism, and their exponents.[26] How and when the deed would follow the promise was merely a matter of time. Therefore the existence of the 'Government' was little more than disguised internment or captivity.[27] The arrests of 23 May 1945 showed – in an unnecessarily vulgar form – the grim reality.[28]

Chapter 3

The Capitulation

After Dönitz, who until then had urged and ordered uncompromising resistance,[1] received the first of the three signals on 30 April, he seemed to one of his closest colleagues to be 'a changed man'.[2] Supported by Speer, who even during Hitler's lifetime had turned his back on the order for wilful destruction and decided instead in favour of saving whatever material remained, and the 'strength of the people',[3] Dönitz declared unequivocally: 'Put an end to it, preserve the substance, no more unnecessary bloodshed, no more senseless destruction.'

Although some in his entourage still believed that a successful military resistance was possible, and over-estimated the local successes of small units, Dönitz had finally admitted that the military situation was 'hopeless'.[4] Schörner (Army Group Centre), Generaloberst Lindemann (Denmark) and General Böhme (Norway), who all favoured fighting on, and were supported in this by the OKW, could not persuade him.[5] He obtained support from Gauleiter Wegener, as well as Schwerin von Krosigk, who had only accepted his new post because Dönitz had entrusted him with the surrender negotiations.[6] All three considered unconditional surrender out of the question, however, because this would expose millions of German soldiers and civilians to Bolshevist atrocities.

For some time it was undecided whether the surrender to the West should be handled by Dönitz or left to individual military leaders.[7] In the latter case this would frustrate the Allied demand for total unconditional surrender,[8] sparing Dönitz a painful task which might also have an unpleasant aftermath in the domestic arena.[9] Schwerin von Krosigk was opposed to this course. So long as the battle was being fought somewhere, the various enemies were justified in continuing to bomb: new devastation of cities in the as-yet unoccupied areas of the Reich and the deaths of thousands of women and children would be the consequence. Above all it was necessary to appear to the Allies to have a fully responsible, central leadership and so defuse any later allegation that German government authority operated in a vacuum. With these observations, Schwerin von Krosigk did no more than confirm Dönitz in his own beliefs.[10] Dönitz had decided to orchestrate a planned surrender by stages under his own direction, and the fact that he brought the war to an end 'officially' as soon as he could became – contrary to his fears – the act for which he will always be remembered in Germany.

Because details of the British operation 'Eclipse' had fallen into German hands, the intended division of Germany into zones was already roughly known:[11] what a Bolshevist occupation would mean, experience had already shown.[12] The first and most pressing concern for the new 'Government' was therefore the evacuation of the greatest possible number of refugees from the East into the future Western zone of occupation, and to prevent German soldiers being taken prisoner by the Russians.[13] The worst decisions of the past could no longer be made good, however: thus Army Group Kurland and the army on the Frische Nehrung were on the whole as good as lost,[14] and only small contingents could still be got away by sea.[15]

Army Group Centre in Bohemia had another option open: if they set out at once, the entire force could fight its way through to the Americans. OKW countermanded the necessary orders to Schörner:[16] the Soviets would mount an armoured attack and quickly transform the retreat into a rout with heavy casualties. This placed Dönitz in a difficult position. Apart from his desire to avoid casualties, it was not clear if the stubborn Schörner would obey his orders before having had the opportunity to present his own plans. Moreover it remained uncertain what had been agreed at Yalta regarding Bohemia, so that any retreat at all might be an unnecessary gamble. Dönitz therefore reserved his decision until he had discussed it with Schörner or his Chief of Staff, but later he regretted the postponement.[17]

The conference, which began at 1700 hrs on 4 May 1945, set the earliest acceptable date for total surrender.[18] Generalleutnant von Natzmer, Schörner's Chief of Staff, replied to the question how long the Army Group would need at the most to reach the American lines with: 'One week'.

Accordingly the reprieve had to last until 11 May. The Americans suspected that this was a tactic to surrender only to the Western Powers and so gain time to drive a wedge between them and the Soviets.[19] Yet although the Germans would gladly have done that, and how justified were their warnings regarding the impending political developments[20] which they addressed to the West, there was no prospect of success. After Hitler had forced the West and the Soviets to combine against him, the former, despite their distrust and bad experiences with the Russians, were not prepared to deal with Germany, which had fought tooth and nail to the last.[21] Moreover, Japan remained undefeated, and the atomic bombs were not ready.[22] Thus all the secret German hopes for a split amongst the Allies were illusory, and nothing remained but to give in to all of them and take the consequences.

In February 1945 while Hitler still lived, at the initiative of General der Waffen-SS Wolff, the most senior SS and police commander in Italy, talks had been held in Switzerland regarding a partial surrender in Italy.[23] After a lull, these led to a secret agreement on 29 April at Field-Marshal Alexander's HQ at Caserta. The surrender of Army Group C (South-west) under Generaloberst von Vietinghoff-Scheel came into effect on 2 May at midday.[24] In contrast to Kesselring and OKW-South, initially opposed to the surrender,[25] Dönitz approved it swiftly because it fitted his overall strategy[26] and this set in motion the entire capitulation process.

From now on events began to roll. The collapse of the Italian front brought heavy pressure on the neighbouring German armies in the north,[27] and on 2 May Army Group G asked Allied HQ where they should turn to discussing surrender.[28] They were referred to General Devers, US 6th Army Group. Meanwhile Kesselring had already been authorised to conclude an armistice there,[29] and on 3 May he took immediate steps to make known in advance the details of the coming cease-fire in order to avoid further fighting and 'senseless bloodshed'.[30] Hopes resting on negotiations to save Army Groups South-East (Löhr), South (Rendulic) and Centre (Schörner) evaporated when the Americans demanded the unconditional surrender of Army Group G. The instrument was signed at Haar near Munich on 4 May and came into effect the next day.[31]

Meanwhile Dönitz had set in train negotiations on his own account. His original intention had been to keep open a gap between Lauenburg and Lübeck to allow refugees and troops to 'flow through' from East to West,[32] but the rapid advance of British forces on 2 May from Lauenburg to Lübeck, and the surprise arrival of the Americans at Wismar via Schwerin, quickly put paid to this idea.[33] Further resistance here was useless, and Dönitz decided to contact the commander-in-chief of the British 21st Army Group officially.[34] The same day he despatched Generaladmiral von Friedeburg with a small delegation to Montgomery's HQ on Lüneburg Heath.[35] This pre-empted an independent action by C-in-C North, Generalfeldmarschall Busch and the Wehrmacht Commander for Denmark, Generaloberst Lindemann, both of whom had made it known through an envoy in Stockholm on 30 April that they would surrender once troops of the Western Allies reached Lübeck.[36] Since General Blumentritt also wished to surrender his army in north-west Germany,[37] Dönitz's decision to offer a centralised capitulation for the entire northern theatre prevented confusion at the fronts and further unnecessary casualties.[38]

Von Friedeburg's offer was neither accepted immediately nor rejected outright.[39] If Montgomery had authority from Allied High Command to accept a military surrender in his operational area as a tactical and local opportunity,[40] for political reasons he could neither grant the German request to accommodate Army Group Vistula behind his lines, nor discuss at all the problem of the German refugees from the East. Instead he proposed the surrender of all German forces in north-west Germany and Schleswig-Holstein including the islands, Holland and Denmark.[41] Because the Field-Marshal also agreed that all German soldiers from the Eastern fronts who surrendered individually to British units would be accepted as British prisoners of war and not turned over to the Soviets, and he did not wish to appear 'inhumane' on the refugee question,[42] once von Friedeburg had submitted his report in person to Dönitz at 1830 hrs on 4 May there was agreement.[46] Since the cease-fire was not scheduled to begin until 0800 hrs German summer time the following day, German military movements continued,[44] and what the Luftwaffe could transfer out was transferred out, while the Kriegsmarine kept its transports sailing. Dönitz ordered that no further destruction was to be undertaken, no ships sunk and the U-boat War was to end.[45]

Resistance continued on the Eastern Front[46] while the fighting in the southern theatre was so effectively united under Kesselring's leadership that in
addition to the troops the greatest possible number of civilians was saved from
the Soviets.[47] Meanwhile von Friedeburg flew to see Eisenhower in Rheims in
order to negotiate further partial surrenders in the West[48] while Kesselring as
Commander-in-Chief West sought approval to despatch a plenipotentiary to
negotiate an armistice.[49] Eisenhower, through his Chief of the Staff Walter
Bedell Smith, was not prepared to discuss anything except unconditional surrender everywhere.[50] It was his point of view that as Allied Commander-in-
Chief he could not accept limited local tactical surrenders. Above all he was
politically constrained much more tightly than Montgomery and feared the
suspicion of the Soviets.[51] Accordingly he expressly informed the latter of his
standpoint and asked for a Soviet representative to attend at the Western HQ
for the coming talks. The Russian High Command thereupon despatched
Major-General Suslaparov to Rheims.[52]

Friedeburg had no authority to comply with Eisenhower's demand, and
thus his companion General Kinzel had to travel back to Dönitz[53] so as not
to break the agreed radio silence. Eisenhower's way out of the dilemma,
handing over to the Russians the German armies in the East and the refugees
from the eastern provinces as an alternative to continuing the fighting, was
never considered by the Germans despite the attempt to bluff them by use of
a map showing faked new 'drives' intended by the Americans and Soviets.[54]

It was still hoped that by being 'completely frank' about the situation the
Americans could be made more accommodating.[55] Jodl was given the job and
the authority to conclude the unconditional surrender, and sent to Rheims on
6 May 1945.[56] In the worst-case scenario he was to attempt to gain a few days
between the cease-fire and the cessation of all movements. He was not to sign
anything without having consulted Dönitz beforehand.

Jodl enjoyed as little success with the victors as had von Friedeburg. Smith
was bound by his instructions and could not see for the life of him why the
Germans did not want to surrender to the Soviets. His sober observation that
the Germans had played for high stakes and lost was certainly difficult to
rebut. He was at least prepared, however, to consider Jodl's proposal to allow
the commanders-in-chief of each Wehrmacht branch to sign the instrument

of capitulation and allow forty-eight hours for the distribution of the necessary orders. This meant that the afternoon of 10 May would be the deadline,
not far short of the period of reprieve aimed for. Unfortunately Eisenhower,
who had been warned of the German negotiating tactic in a telephone call
from Montgomery's HQ the previous day,[57] would not hear of it, and insisted
that the capitulation should be signed on 6 May, but agreed to delay its
coming into effect until a minute past midnight on 9 May German summer
time. If not, he would resume the bomber offensive and close the British and
American lines to Germans fleeing from the East.[58] Jodl was offered half an
hour to think it over, but decided instead to signal Keitel requesting permission to sign.[59] There was a delay before the answer came because Dönitz was
not shown the signal until after midnight. He saw himself as compelled to
agree, and at 0241 hrs on 7 May 1945 in the presence of Eisenhower's Chief
of Staff, the Soviet representative at Allied HQ and a French witness, Jodl
signed the instrument.[60]

The document handed over all German fighting forces on land, sea and in
the air in all theatres of war unconditionally to the Supreme Commander of
the Allied Expeditionary Forces and the Soviet High Command. Eisenhower
made Jodl personally responsible for the observance of the terms.[61] A bare
forty-eight hours had been gained to save the people in the East, time which
it was now imperative to use.[62]

At Eisenhower's instigation the formal signing had to be repeated on 8 May
1945 in Berlin in a ceremony for the benefit of the Soviets. It sprang from his
'crusader' mentality and political naïveté in which he thought it necessary to
'symbolise the unity of the Western Allies and the Soviets' and to make clear
to the Germans in as drastic manner as possible that they had not only surrendered to the Western Powers.[63] Thus at Rheims, Jodl was obliged to appear
with Keitel and the commanders-in-chief of the Wehrmacht branches at a
place and time to be determined by Eisenhower and the Soviet High
Command for the formal ratification of the document.[64]

The Western Powers contented themselves with the role of invited guests.
Air Marshal Tedder, General Spaatz and General de Lattre de Tassigny were
the Western representatives with Marshal Zhukov, who presided at the ceremony. Keitel as OKW Chief and the highest ranking officer led the German

delegation. Since there had been no effective Army Commander-in-Chief since Hitler's death Keitel also took on this role while Generaloberst Stumpff deputised as the most easily-reached senior Luftwaffe officer in place of the wounded Commander-in-Chief Ritter von Greim. Only the Kriegsmarine was represented by its actual Commander-in-Chief, Generaladmiral von Friedeburg.[65]

On the morning of 8 May the delegation flew from Flensburg to Stendal, where a new flight commanded by Air Marshal Tedder, Eisenhower's representative, was on hand.[66] The party landed at Tempelhof and was driven to the old Pioneer Training Camp at Karlshorst, arriving at 1300 hrs. Keitel had been given the German-language version of the instrument at the airfield and after comparing it to the Rheims original made a few minor alterations.[67] The only important introduction had been new penalties for troops who failed to hand over their weapons. Keitel objected and demanded a guarantee that no disciplinary measures would be taken until twenty-four hours after the corresponding German orders had been issued. Zhukov agreed to twelve hours. This cleared away all German objections to signing, but the German delegation was then herded into a small villa near the military school to wait out the hours until midnight, when the capitulation came into effect. At the appropriate time Keitel and his party were led into the hall. The signing of the four copies seemed to the Germans to 'last an eternity' and dragged on until somewhere towards 0200 hrs. Nevertheless, the date on the document was left at 8 May 1945.[68] Thus did Hitler's total war end officially in total defeat and unconditional surrender.[69]

The serious work of the Dönitz Government bore no fruit even though the first discussions between Dönitz and the U.S. General Rooks aboard the *Patria* on 13 May were encouraging.[70] This plenipotentiary of Eisenhower apparently had sympathy for the need of a central authority and promised to work along the lines Dönitz was proposing. At that time the Admiral did not have the impression that the end of his Government was imminent, even if he considered its purpose 'limited as to time and extent'.[71] Proposals for future collaboration with the various Allied headquarters were submitted and further detailed files on transport and supply prepared.[72] Jodl, successor as head of OKW to the arrested Keitel, even looked to the future with great optimism. He felt 'a calling to master even the greatest tasks'.[73] Lacking a working apparatus for administration, at least the question of supply had to be worked out initially by the Wehrmacht, from which the 'Government' received technical instructions.[74]

The most senior Allied political authorities decided otherwise. The details of what went on amongst the victors is presently impossible to say exactly. That the Germans were to be 'shielded from the Russian thirst for knowledge' after a Soviet commission under Major-General Truskov went to Flensburg on 17 May is doubtful,[75] but the fear of the Western Allies that the Germans might turn to the East may have accelerated the demise of the Dönitz Government.[76] The alternative idea, that they were arrested 'at Stalin's behest' is unsupported by any evidence.[77] The only certainty is the remorse-less dedication of the United States to faithfully upholding the earlier agreement about Germany – vague as it was – and going along with the demands of the Soviets.[78]

Churchill, substantially more far-sighted than Truman and his advisors, did not get his way.[79] He was less anxious to hear out the international control authority within which the Bolshevists were pursuing their own agenda[80] but the Americans insisted, from apparent concern at the rapid 'economic and social collapse' in Germany, on having the other victorious Powers approve the proclamation on the German defeat drafted on 22 May 1945 by the European Advisory Commission so that it could be ceremonially published by the four commanders-in-chief at the beginning of June in Berlin.[81] This would bring into being the Allied Control Council, and thus the fate of the Dönitz Government was sealed.

Chapter 4

Finis Germaniae? The Reich as a Problem of International and Constitutional Law

When the American commandant of Mondorf Camp proclaimed to the assembled prisoners on 7 July 1945 that 'the German State has ceased to exist'[1] he was probably acting under orders with which he found himself in agreement. The opening sentences of the Allied declaration of 5 June 1945, in which the victors assumed formally 'supreme Government power', speak of 'Germany's unconditional surrender' as the alleged basis of their right.[2] It was supposed to appear as if the Reich as such in Rheims and Berlin had delivered itself up: Finis germaniae.

To impute this sense to the phrase 'unconditional surrender'[3] and to couple the military surrender to a political one in international and constitutional law was the original Allied programme.[4] What was to be inflicted on the Germans legally, and extracted from them under the pressure of defeat, was something different, however. The confusing and confused plans of the victors for the treatment of the Reich after the war reflect the tensions amongst them and the differences in their own houses.

The story of the would-be treaty, a daughter of the 1919 Treaty of Versailles, which was to be the result of the past policy and basis of the future policy, has its tragi-comic aspect,[5] for at the moment when the Germans were ready to capitulate, all the work went to waste. It had been agreed at the Moscow Foreign Ministers' Conference between 28 October and 1 November 1943 to found a European Advisory Commission in London whose duties would involve 'examining European questions arising in connection with the termination of hostilities and to make corresponding recommendations to the three Governments'.[6] The initial meeting was held at Lancaster House in London on 14 January 1944[7] and resulted in 'the decisive – and also only – instrument for the preparation and determination of Allied post-war policy in Germany'. The first step was a proposal as to how the Reich was to be handled when defeated. The Governments were presented with a report on 25 July 1944 to which was attached the draft of an instrument for the 'Unconditional Capitulation of Germany'.[8] After France had joined the Commission on 27 November 1944, their representative also received a copy and – after the French had approved it, and it had been accepted by them upon their becoming a signatory Power on 1 May 1945 – it remained basically unaltered awaiting VE Day.

Meanwhile a second version had seen the light of day after a supplement at Yalta at the Soviet instigation was added which spoke of the 'dismemberment of Germany'.[9] Because Stalin refused to have France on the Dismemberment Committee, the French could not be put in the picture, and a consensus as to which text should be given to the Germans had not been reached at the time of the German collapse. All attempts by the US representative Winant for the matter to be clarified in the first days of May were met by the obstinate silence of the Soviets. Several copies of the two versions were kept ready in London for all eventualities, but in vain.[10]

The US generals at Eisenhower's HQ solved the problem in their own way.[11] As soldiers they had little time for diplomatic scribblers and considered the document 'too long and legalistic'. What they wanted was simply a fast and if possible uncomplicated end to hostilities. This aim would no doubt have been delayed by the necessary porings over the constitutional clauses of the wording, and so Eisenhower's Chief of Staff was happy to have no copy of either version available at the time of the capitulation negotiations.[12] 'Therefore down to work,' declared Walter Bedell Smith, and drew up a document of purely military character. Churchill, warned by a watchful official, telephoned the general and asked why no stipulations regarding the transfer of sovereignty to the Allies had been included. Smith quickly interpolated the famous, or notorious, Clause 4 that appeared in the Lüneburg instrument and reserved the right of the victors to invoke further unstipulated measures towards 'Germany' and the Wehrmacht if they so wished. The allegedly far-sighted plans for a common victors' post-war policy began with ambiguity and shady dealings that could not be overcome subsequently.

The documents signed in Rheims and Berlin were by their contents a formal military surrender. Even the term 'capitulation' is purely military in the generally recognised sphere of international law.[13] The entire set-up at Rheims and Berlin proved the same thing: the soldiers of both sides negotiated and signed: they acted 'in the name of' their High Commands and the document was accordingly entitled 'An Act of Military Surrender'.[14] The 'elastic' Clause 4, probably signed without hesitation by the Germans, held open the possibility to inflict upon the Reich at some later time perhaps some general surrender terms of a political nature through the 'United Nations' or in their name.[15] This remains open at the time of writing [i.e. 1964].

Not even the fact that the Wehrmacht capitulated 'unconditionally' gave the victors the right to act as they liked. The term 'unconditional surrender' originated in the American Civil War and is not a term recognised in international law.[16] Attempts to transform the Second World War into an 'international civil war' were doomed to fail because the Allies themselves did not want the idea on the grounds that they were not prepared to exempt the German Resistance from Germany's overall war guilt. Efforts in retrospect to declare the formula as *ad hoc* valid international law found no serious takers.[17] It was moreover an obstacle to the official aim of the victors to create a world order of laws in which arbitrariness had no place. Finally, 'unconditional surrender' is a contradiction in terms, for a declaration of will to have no will in future is a violation in principle of the essence and idea of what a treaty is.[18] Future absence of will and intent can only be enforced by force.

After Stalin, following a tactical shift of opinion, had declared that 'Hitler come or go, the German State, the German people will remain'[19] in the Berlin Four-Power proclamation of 5 June 1945, the Allies reiterated that their taking the reins of power in Germany would not bring about 'the annexation of Germany'.[20] Likewise the Potsdam Agreement confirmed the existence of the German State in law, considering it as a future peaceable nation after certain conditions were fulfilled.[21] Even if the theory of an effective destruction of a state in the form of a 'condominium', i.e. the subjection of the Reich into the sovereignty of the victor state without annexation,[22] or through so-called subjugation, is ruled out. All theories in this direction are disputed or opposed today in international law.[23]

As time went on the view gained ground that even though the Third Reich ended with the capitulation of 8 May 1945 and the Allied declaration of 5 June 1945, i.e. that a particular regime and its operators were removed, nevertheless despite temporary restriction of its sovereignty, despite inability to act and losses of all territories acquired after 31 December 1937, the German Reich as then constituted remained intact.

The complex problem of 'Germany' has become insoluble in international law of late because no higher authority exists to determine what is just.[24] It seems as if in future only a political solution is possible, which then, following tradition, must give rise to a new legal construction provided with peaceful endurance.[25] In its constitution and effect, despite all its efforts, the Dönitz Government was less the beginning of a new state than the end of the old one. Nevertheless it must be clearly acknowledged that Dönitz was installed without previous preparation in a desperate situation that he mastered in his own way. The carefully engineered, rapid end to the war will be his enduring monument. To have continued the fighting and destruction of property to total exhaustion would perhaps have made reconstruction impossible.[26] From the military and political point of view, Dönitz probably had no leeway to act in a manner different to the way he did. Whether he should have 'rethought' his personal situation, i.e. clearly distanced himself from National Socialism, is another matter. He did not succeed in outjumping his shadow...

Appendices

The Appendices are an attempt to provide a documentary foundation for the text, and include the various proclamations issued regarding the problems of the time. The author has consciously limited the selection of material to the era involved and the subject matter under discussion. Unfortunately the quest for, and assembly of, the material ran into serious personal and technical difficulties, which could not always be overcome. Former Gauleiter Wegener, acting as Secretary of State in the Dönitz Government, had the task of collecting and safeguarding the important papers of the time, but we were permanently deprived of this collection once in captivity. Accordingly I had had to rely on copies we managed to keep and – in some cases – on extracts from contemporary newspapers insofar as there exists no doubt of their provenance or accuracy.

I was able to check and complete Appendix 3 with the kind co-operation of the Bundesarchiv at Koblenz.

Professor Georg Erler
Spring 1964

Appendix 1

Extract from Hitler's Speech to the Reichstag, Friday 1 September 1939

'… I have therefore donned once more that tunic which is most holy and precious to me. I shall not cast it aside until victory is won, or I shall not survive the end! Should anything happen to me during this struggle, Party Member Göring is my immediate successor. Should anything happen to Party Member Göring, the next successor in line is Party Member Hess. You would be bound to these as Führer with that same blind faith and obedience as you are to me. In the event that anything should happen to Party Member Hess, I am now calling upon the Senate for a law whereby the most worthy man, that is to say the bravest man, shall be chosen from amongst you.'

Source: Report of the Sittings of the German Reichstag, Vol 460, pp 45ff.

Appendix 2

Power of Plenipotentiary for the Preparation of the Defence of the Northern Region

The Führer
Berlin 20 April 1945

I give the Commander in Chief of the Navy the task of preparing immediately all measures necessary involving personnel and materials for the defence of the Northern Region in the event that communication by land with Central Germany is cut off. I provide him with power of plenipotentiary to issue order to all centres of the State, Party and Wehrmacht in the Region for this purpose.

Signed: Adolf Hitler

Source: Bundesarchiv, Collection R62/10.

Appendix 3

Hitler's Political Testament

Eagle and swastika insignia
Adolf Hitler

MY POLITICAL TESTAMENT

Thirty years have now passed since I contributed my modest abilities in 1914 as a volunteer in the First World War, forced upon the Reich.

In these three decades, all my ideas, actions and my life have been dominated by love of and loyalty to my people. They gave me the strength to take those most difficult decisions never previously confronting a mortal being. I have used up my time, and lost my physical strength and my health in those three decades.

It is not true that I or anybody else in Germany wanted war in 1939. It was wanted and set in train exclusively by those international statesmen who were either of Jewish origin or working for Jewish interests. I have made too many offers for arms limitation and limited disarmament, which posterity will never be able to deny, for anybody to place the blame for this war on my shoulders.

After the First World War I never wanted a second war against Britain or even the United States. Centuries will pass but from the ruins of our cities and monuments hate will be renewed against the people who are, when all is said and done, responsible, and to whom we are indebted for everything: international Jewry and its helpers!

Three days before the outbreak of the German-Polish war I suggested to the British ambassador to Berlin a solution for the German-Polish problem similar to the case of the Saar region, under international supervision. This offer can also not be denied. It was only rejected because the decisive circles in British politics wanted war, partly for the hoped-for business accruing from it, partly motivated by a propaganda campaign set up by international Jewry.

I left people in no doubt that if the peoples of Europe were seen only as the share portfolios of these money and financial conspirators, then those responsible would be brought to account, and they are the real culprits in this murderous struggle: Jewry! Nor did I leave people in any doubt but that this time millions of men would not die and hundreds of thousands of women and children would not be bombed and burnt to death in the cities without the real guilty party having to atone for its guilt, if by more humane means.

After a six-year struggle which despite all the defeats will go down in history as the most glorious and valorous proof of a people's will to exist, I cannot be apart from the city which is the capital of the Reich. Since our forces are too small to hold off the enemy assault here, and the resistance is gradually being whittled away by their unseeing automatons, I desire to share my fate with the millions of others who are remaining in this city. Moreover I shall not fall into the hands of the enemy to provide a show organised by the Jews for the pleasure of their frenzied masses.

I am therefore resolved to stay in Berlin where of my own free will I shall choose to die at that moment when I consider the office of Führer and Chancellor can no longer be defended. I die with a heart joyful at the deeds beyond measure, and achievements of our men at the front, of our women at home, of the accomplishments of our farmers and workers, and the unique military involvement in history of our Youth which bears my name.

That I express to them my thanks from the bottom of my heart is as self-evident as my wish that under no circumstances should they abandon the struggle but, irrespective of venue, should continue it against the enemies of the Fatherland, in the manner of the great Clausewitz.

From the sacrifice of our fighting men and my own identification with them unto death, sooner or later in Germany a seed will sprout for the gleaming rebirth of the National Socialist Movement and with it the realisation of a true ethnic-German community.

Many of the bravest men and women have decided to bind their lives to mine to the end. I have begged them and finally ordered them not to do this but to participate in a continuation of the nation's struggle. I request the commanders of the armies, the Navy and the Luftwaffe to employ the most exhaustive measures to stiffen our soldiers' will to resist in the National Socialist sense and I refer especially to the fact that as the founder and creator of this Movement I have myself preferred death to cowardly running away or capitulation. May it become a point of honour of the Army officer one day – as is already the case with our Navy – that the surrender of a territory or a city is out of the question and that above all the commanders must set a shining example by their devotion to duty unto death.

POLITICAL TESTAMENT – Second Part

Before my death I expel from the Party the former Reichsmarschall Hermann Göring and deprive him of all rights arising from the Edict of 29 June 1941 and my Reichstag declaration of 1 September 1939. In his place I appoint Grossadmiral Dönitz as Reich President and Supreme Commander of the Wehrmacht.

Before my death I expel from the Party and from all State offices the former Reichsführer-SS and Reich Interior Minister Heinrich Himmler. In his place I appoint Gauleiter Karl Hanke as Reichsführer-SS and Chief Officer of the German Police, and Gauleiter Paul Giesler as Reich Interior Minister.

By negotiating secretly with the enemy, without my knowledge and against my will, and by their attempts to seize power for themselves in the State unlawfully, Göring and Himmler have inflicted immeasurable harm on the country and the whole population, quite apart from the disloyalty to my person.

In order to provide the German people with a Government composed of honourable men who will fulfil their obligation to prosecute the war with all means at their disposal, I appoint as leaders of the nation the following members to the new Cabinet:

Reich President: Dönitz
Reich Chancellor: Goebbels
Party Minister: Bormann
Foreign Minister: Seyss-Inquart
Minister of Interior: Gauleiter Giesler
War Minister: Dönitz
C-in-C Army: Schörner
C-in-C Kriegsmarine: Dönitz
C-in-C Luftwaffe: Greim
Reichsführer-SS and Chief, German Police Gauleiter Hanke
Economy: Funk
Agriculture: Backe
Justice: Thierach
Culture: Dr Scheel

Propaganda: Dr Naumann
Finance: Schwerin von Krosigk
Labour: Dr Hupfauer
Armaments: Saur
Leader of the German Workers' Front and Member of the Reich Cabinet:
    Reich Minister Dr Ley.

Although a number of these men such as Martin Bormann, Dr Goebbels etc and their wives came to me voluntarily and were desirous of not leaving the Reich capital under any circumstances, but were prepared to go under with me, I must nevertheless ask them to obey my instructions and in this case put the interests of the nation above their own feelings.

By their work and devotion they will remain close to me as my companions in equal measure after my death, and as I hope, my spirit will remain among them and accompany them always. May they be hard but never unjust, may they above all never allow fear to be the arbiter of their dealings, and put the honour of the nation above everything on Earth. Finally may they be conscious that our task of expanding a National Socialist State is the work of the coming years and obliges every individual to always serve the common interest, and relegate his own interests. I demand of all Germans, of all National Socialist men and women, and all servicemen of the Wehrmacht that they be faithful and obedient to the new Government and to its President unto death.

Above all I bind the leaders of the nation and those they lead to the strict observance of the racial laws and uncompromising resistance to the poisoner of all the worlds' peoples, international Jewry.

Dictated in Berlin, 29 April 1945, 0400 hrs
Adolf Hitler

As witnesses: Dr Joseph Goebbels, Martin Bormann, Wilhelm Burgdorf, Hans Krebs.

Source: From Max Domarus, *ibid*, pp 2236–9: the text above in translation conforms to the original German text as photocopied from the Nuremberg IMT documentation, 1.Ex, Nuremberg State Archive.

GOEBBELS' ATTACHMENT TO HITLER'S TESTAMENT

The Führer has ordered me to leave the Reich capital Berlin in the event that the defence fails, and to take part as a senior member in the Government appointed by him. For the first time in my life I must categorically refuse to obey an order of the Führer. My wife and my children associate themselves with this refusal. First, for humanitarian grounds and out of personal loyalty, we would never be able to desert the Führer in his darkest hour: secondly it would always seem to me to be a dishonourable act, and for the rest of my life I would think of myself as having ratted on him, I would lose my self-respect and the respect of the people.

I believe I would best serve the future of the people by remaining, for in the hard times ahead the memory of a man will be more important than the man himself. For this reason I express the irrevocable resolve of myself and my wife not to leave the Reich capital and instead bring to an end at the Führer's side a life that for me personally has no further value if I cannot lead it in the service of the Führer and beside him.
Berlin 29 Apr 1945 0530hrs. Signed, Dr Goebbels.

Source: From: Domarus, *ibid*, p 2241, note 213.

MY PRIVATE TESTAMENT

I considered it irresponsible to marry during the years of political struggle. Therefore before ending my earthly span I have now resolved to take to my wife that woman who, after long years of faithful friendship, came of her own free will to the then almost beleaguered city in order to share my fate. At her own insistence she will die with me as my spouse. It will restore to us what my work in the service of my people stole from us both.

Whatever I own – insofar as it has any value – belongs to the Party: if this ceases to exist, then to the State. Should the State also be destroyed, no further decision of mine is necessary. I have collected the paintings bought by myself over the years not for private purposes, but to develop an art gallery in my home city of Linz/Danube. It is my most heartfelt wish that this legacy should be carried through. As executor I nominate my most loyal Party member Martin Bormann. He is authorised to make all decisions in the role of final and legal arbiter. He may allocate anything of personal value as a souvenir or for the necessities of a lower middle-class life for my sisters, equally and above all for the mother of my wife and to my male and female secretaries, Frau Winter etc., known to him and who have supported me for years by their work.

My wife and I choose death to avoid the ignominy of fleeing or capitulating. It is our wish that our bodies be burnt immediately afterwards in that place where I have carried out the greater part of my daily work in the course of 12 years' service to my people.

Signed, Adolf Hitler

As witnesses: Martin Bormann, Dr Goebbels. As witness: Nikolaus von Below.

Source: Domarus, *ibid*, pp 2240–1.

Appendix 4

Telex Message from Dönitz to Gauleiter Kaufmann, late on 30 April 1945.

In reply to your telex of 30 April I would reply as follows:

1. The main concern of the German leadership in the current situation is to hold German territory and spare the German population from Bolshevism. The focus of our operations is therefore unequivocally in the East. Everything militarily possible will be done to halt the Russian advance in the Mecklenburg region or at least detain it as long as we can to enable Germans to flow out.
2. This outflow will only be possible while a gateway to the West remains open over the border between the occupation zones agreed at Yalta. If the Elbe-Trave Canal is closed down by the British, seven million valuable Germans will be sacrificed to the whim of the Russians.

3. It is therefore absolutely necessary to defend the Elbe position against the West with the utmost tenacity. Where property is destroyed as a result of military necessity, this will be justified a thousand times over by the saving of German blood in the East. It is not intended to carry out intensive destruction of harbour or industrial installations, and this must be prevented at all costs.
4. By your unreserved support for the foregoing military objectives, you and the city of Hamburg can make the best contribution in the struggle for the destiny of our people.

Heil Hitler!
Dönitz, Grossadmiral.

Source: Original in the State archive, Hamburg. The telex bears the reference 'KRMBGL 770 30/42100' which means it was sent at 2100 hrs (according to kind information supplied by the Hamburg Senate, State Archive, 21 July 1964).

Appendix 5

Signals Regarding the Death of Hitler and the Appointment of Dönitz

First Signal
Sent Berlin 30 Apr 1945 1807 hrs
Logged Plön 30 Apr 1945 1835 hrs

'For Grossadmiral Dönitz. In place of the former Reichsmarschall "Göring", the Führer named you, Herr Grossadmiral, as his successor. Full powers in writing on way to you. With immediate effect you are authorised to take all measures appropriate to the present situation. Bormann.'

Second Signal
Sent Berlin 1 May 1945 0745 hrs
Logged Plön 1 May 1945 1053 hrs

'For Grossadmiral Dönitz. (Senior Officer Matter!) Testament in force. I will come to you soonest. Until then in my opinion withhold publication. Bormann.'

Third Signal
Sent Berlin 1 May 1945 1446 hrs
Logged Plön 1 May 1945 1518 hrs.

'For Grossadmiral Dönitz. (Senior Officer Matter. Only by Officer!) Führer deceased yesterday 1530 hrs. Testament dated 29.4.1945 bestows upon you office of Reich President, upon Reich Minister Goebbels the office of Reich Chancellor, upon Reichsleiter Bormann the office of Minister for the Party, upon Reich Minister Seyss-Inquart the office of Reich Foreign Minister. By order of the Führer the Testament has been brought out of Berlin to you, to Feldmarschall Schörner and to a safe place for the public. Reichsleiter Bormann is attempting to reach you today to report on the situation. The manner and time of the announcement to the forces and public left to you. Confirm receipt. Goebbels, Bormann.'

Source: Original with cypher files, Bundesarchiv, Collection R62/8.

Appendix 6

Radio Broadcast announcing Hitler's Death

Sender Hamburg 1 May 1945 22.26 hrs

'It is reported from Führer-HQ that our Führer Adolf Hitler fell for Germany this afternoon at his command post in the Reich Chancellery. He fought against Bolshevism to his last breath. On 30 April the Führer appointed Grossadmiral Dönitz as his successor.'

Source: Extract from Document D-444 (Exhibit No. GB188, British prosecuting authority, Nuremberg. *Flensburger Nachrichten*, Issue 102, 2 May 1945.

Appendix 7a

Dönitz Broadcasts to the German People, 1 May 1945

'German men and women, soldiers of the German Wehrmacht! Our Führer Adolf Hitler has fallen. The German people bow their heads in deepest mourning and respect. At an early stage he had recognised the terrible menace of Bolshevism and dedicated his life to opposing it. At the end of his struggle and unerring straight path, he died a hero in the capital of the German Reich. His life was a unique service for Germany. His war against the Bolshevist flood was fought for Europe and the whole civilised world.

'The Führer appointed me his successor. Conscious of the responsibility I accept the leadership of the German people in this fateful hour. It is my first duty to save the German populace from annihilation by the advancing Bolshevist enemy. We fight on simply for this reason. So long as, and insofar as, this objective is impeded by the British and Americans, we shall continue to defend ourselves against them and fight them. The Anglo-Americans would then be prosecuting the war not for their own peoples, but only for the expansion of Bolshevism in Europe. What the German people achieved and suffered in the Homeland in fighting this war is unique in history. In the dark days ahead, to the extent that it is in my power, I shall strive to create tolerable living conditions for our brave men, women and children.

'For that I need your help. Give me your trust, for your path is also my path. Uphold order and discipline in the cities and provinces, everybody must do his duty at his post! Only in that way can we reduce the suffering which the days ahead are going to bring us all, and prevent the collapse. If we do everything in our power, the Lord God will not desert us after so much suffering and sacrifice.'

Source: Bundesarchiv, Collection R62/2: *Flensburger Nachrichten* No. 102, 2 May 1945.

Appendix 7b

Dönitz's Order of the Day to the Wehrmacht, 1 May 1945

'German Wehrmacht! My comrades! The Führer has fallen. Faithful to his great idea to preserve the people of Europe against Bolshevism, he committed his life to it and died a hero's death. We have lost one of the greatest heroes in German history. In proud respect and mourning we lower our flags before him.

'The Führer named me his successor as Head of State and Supreme Commander of the Wehrmacht. I assume command of all Arms of service of the German Wehrmacht with the objective of continuing the war against the Bolshevists until our fighting troops and hundreds of thousands of families from the East of Germany have been saved from enslavement or annihilation. I must continue the war against Great Britain and the United States for so long as and insofar as they hinder the prosecution of the war against the Bolshevists.

'The situation demands of you, who have already achieved such great historical feats and now yearn for an end to this war, further unconditional commitment. I demand discipline and obedience. Only by the execution of my orders without any reservations can chaos and disaster be avoided. That man is a coward and a traitor who precisely now abandons his duty and therefore causes the death or enslavement of German women and children.

'For each of you the oath of loyalty sworn by you to the Führer is now transferred to me as the Führer's nominated successor. German soldiers, do your duty! The life of our people is at stake.'

Source: Original statement, Bundesarchiv Collection R62/11: Dönitz's address in hand-written form.

Appendix 8

Introduction of the Capitulation in the Northern Region (Telephoned Order from OKW, evening 2 May 1945 to Commandant for the Defence of Hamburg)

1. In order to spare the city and population from total destruction, it is intended not to defend Hamburg.
2. Therefore in accordance with the British offer, on 3 May 0800 hrs a negotiator will be sent with full powers to agree:

    a) Hamburg will not be defended
    b) German forces will cross the Elbe without engaging in hostilities. Simultaneous with this negotiator an OKW delegation will be sent, to be announced today. It will consist of two admirals, one general and aides in four motor vehicles. The delegation has the task of discussing other matters. The agreement to receive this delegation on the morning of 3 May by Keitel, Generalfeldmarschall

Source: Original: Hamburg State Archive.

Appendix 9

Broadcast by Graf Schwerin von Krosigk, 2 May 1945

'German Men and Women!

Grossadmiral Dönitz, whom the Führer named as his successor, has given me the portfolio of Reich Foreign Minister. In Germany's darkest hour I now turn to the public. The world still hears the sounds of war, German men are still dying in the last battles to defend the German homeland. Along the highways of German territory as yet unoccupied, a stream of desperate, starving people hunted by fighter-bombers heads westwards, fleeing from an unspeakable terror, from murder and rape. In the East the Iron Curtain is ever advancing and behind it, hidden from the eyes of the world, the work of exterminating those who have fallen into Bolshevik hands goes on.

In San Francisco talks are being held to debate the organisation of a new world order to indemnify humanity against a new war. The world knows that a Third World War would not mean just the destruction of one nation, but the end of the human race. The terrible weapons not used in this war would appear in a Third World War, bringing death and destruction to the whole world. We Germans, of all peoples of the Earth, have had more experience than any other nation of what war means in its destruction of all culture. Our cities are destroyed, our cultural monuments of Dresden and Nuremberg, Cologne and Bayreuth and other cities of world renown of the German spiritual creation lie in ruins, our cathedrals have become victims of the bombing.

Hundreds of thousands of women and children have been forced to flee before the fury of war, while millions of our German youth and men have fallen at the fronts. If therefore from the hearts of distressed women and mothers the prayer reaches heaven that the world may be saved from the cruel horror of a new war, then it is at its strongest and most heartfelt within the German people. Together with us, all European lands threatened with starvation and the Bolshevist terror hope for a reorganisation which will bring to this part of the Earth, churned over by war, a real and lasting peace, and the possibility of a free and secure life.

But the more that the German East, which is the basic food source for the starving millions in the West, falls into the hands of the Bolshevists, the quicker and more dreadful will be the famine over all Europe. In the despair this need engenders, Bolshevism will flourish. A Communist Europe is the first stage on the path to the Soviet world revolution upon which they deliberately set their sights twenty-five years ago. It is an inescapable consequence of their aims that either they will achieve their goal or there will be a Third World War.

In San Francisco we do not see the fulfilment of what anxious humanity desires. We also believe that a world order must come which will not only prevent future wars but make a timely intervention to extinguish those fires from which wars originate. Such a world order cannot be created, however, if the Red arsonists also sit in judgement in peacetime.

The world can only find peace if the Bolshevist tide does not flood Europe. In a heroic struggle without parallel, for four years Germany fought to its last reserves of strength as Europe's bulwark, and that of the world, against the Red flood. Germany could have saved Europe from Bolshevism if she had had her back free.

Just as it yearns for outward peace, humanity desires internal peace, the solution of the burning social questions in all countries. This solution cannot be found in Bolshevism, but only in a just social order which respects the freedom and dignity of mankind. We honestly believe that we made a contribution towards solving this question when we demonstrated that unemployment and crises can be overcome under the most onerous economic circumstances, and by creating in our State just and dignified work and living conditions for our workers, thus depriving Bolshevism of the ground on which it feeds.

At this moment the world stands on the threshold of the most fateful decisions in history. Depending on how they are resolved, the result will be either chaos or order, war or peace, life or death.'

Source: Bundesarchiv, Collection R62/10.

Appendix 10

Dönitz's Address to the U-boat Arm Upon Abandoning the U-boat Campaign, 4 May 1945

'My U-boat Men! Six years of U-boat warfare lie behind us. You have fought like lions. A crushing material superiority has compressed us into a narrow region. On the basis of what remains it is no longer possible to continue our struggle.

U-boat Men! After a heroic fight without parallel you lay down your arms unbroken and untarnished. We remember with reverence our fallen comrades who sealed their loyalty to Führer and Fatherland with death.

Comrades! Preserve your U-boat spirit, with which you fought through the long years so bravely, tenaciously and unerringly, for the benefit of our Fatherland in the future.

Long live Germany!
Your Grossadmiral.

Source: Bundesarchiv collection R62/2: *Flensburger Nachrichten* No 106, 7 May 1945.

Appendix 11

Instrument of Surrender

See Plate 8.

Photocopy of the original document, from US National Archives Publication No 46-4, Washington DC, 1945, p 7.

Appendix 12

OKW Order to Capitulate in Northern Region

'With effect from 5 May 1945 0800 hrs German summer time, armistice with troops of Field-Marshal Montgomery. This includes all units of the Army, Kriegsmarine, Luftwaffe and Waffen-SS in the regions of the Netherlands, Frisia including the West- and East-Frisian islands and Heligoland, Schleswig-Holstein and Denmark. Ensure troops have received order. Troops will remain in position under arms. Kriegsmarine transport movements already at sea will continue course. No destruction, sinkings of ships or public announcements. Secure all supplies. Discipline and obedience to be maintained with iron rigidity. Further orders follow.

Signed Keitel.'
Source: OKW Führungsstab, Nr 003007/45 g.Kdos 4 May 1945. Copy of this order according to Chief. Mar.Rüstung B.Nr 2675/45 g.Kdos 5 May 1945 (photocopy with author).

Appendix 13

OKW Ordinance to the Capitulation in Northern Region

HQ, 5 May 1945.
From the Supreme Commander of the Wehrmacht: Head OKW/Head Group

To be sent by telex to (1) C-in-C North West (2) Wehrmacht Commander, Denmark (3) C-in-C Netherlands (4) OKM 1/Seekriegsleitung (5) OKL Luftwaffe Command Staff (6) inform Reichsführer-SS (7) inform RAD leadership (8) inform Reichsminister Speer

1. When we lay down our weapons in North-West Germany, Denmark and Holland, we do so because the struggle against the Western Powers has become pointless. In the East, however, the struggle continues in order that we save as many Germans as possible from sovietization and slavery.
2. Every soldier, especially every officer, must ensure by a proud, manly and dignified bearing that the shield of honour of the German nation, even now after almost six years of heroic and honourable battle without equal in world history, remains pure and unstained. Only in that manner can we stand before the victims of this war and uphold their memory in honour. Only so can we help the Homeland in this difficult hour and gain the enemy's respect to which our brave and valiant soldiers have had a right at all times.

3. Weapons are not to be surrendered until the enemy demands it, and then in an orderly manner and jointly.

4. All arsenals, fuel-, provisions- and other dumps and military installations are to be specially guarded by squads under the command of officers to be appointed, and protected against looting. They are not to be surrendered to the enemy until he demands it.

5. The secure and rapid transmission of signals to all subordinated troop units, command posts and military authorities must be absolutely guaranteed.

6. The ordered movements to Denmark (Chef OKW/Chefgruppe Nr 3015/45 g.Kdos 4 May 1945) continue in force.

7. This order applies by analogy to organisations associated with the Wehrmacht (Org.Todt and RAD). The military authorities are responsible for its transmission to them.

8. I make the commanding officers and commanders of all ranks personally responsible for the rapid and conscientious execution of this order.

By Order of:

Signed Keitel, Generalfeldmarschall.
OKW/WFSt 0010004/45 g.Kdos.

Source: Text according to 1SKl 1026/45. Militärgeschichtliches Forschungsamt, Freiburg. The date at para 6. is incorrect, the order referred to was dated 4 Apr 1945. Author).

Appendix 14

Instrument of the Military Capitulation (Rheims, 7 May 1945)

1. The Undersigned, acting in the name of the German High Command, hereby declares the unconditional surrender to the Supreme Commander, Allied Expeditionary Forces and simultaneously to the Soviet Forces High Command, of all forces on land, sea and in the air under German control at this time.

2. The German High Command will transmit orders forthwith to all German command posts of its land, naval and air forces, and to all forces under German control, to cease hostilities at 2301 hrs Central European Time on 8 May and remain in the positions they occupy at that hour. No ship, aircraft or dirigible may be disabled, nor any damage inflicted to the hull of any ship or aircraft, its machinery or equipment.
3. The German High Command will contact the commanders in question immediately to ensure the execution of all further instructions issued by the Supreme Commander of the Allied Expeditionary Forces and the Soviet Forces' High Command.
4. This instrument of military surrender is without prejudice to its replacement by a general instrument of surrender imposed by and in the name of the United Nations (on) Germany and the German forces in their totality.
5. In the event that the German High Command or any of the forces under its control act in a manner contrary to this instrument of surrender, the Supreme Commander of the Allied Expeditionary Forces and the Soviet Forces High Command will take such measures as appear appropriate to them or proceed in another manner.

Signed at Rheims, France at 0241 hrs, this 7th day of May 1945
In the name of the German High Command
Jodl

In the presence of:
In the name of the Supreme Commander of the Allied Expeditionary Forces
W.B.Smith
In the name of the High Command of the Soviet Forces High Command
Sousloparov

F.Sevez
Major-General, French Army (Witness)

Source: Friedrich Klein, *Neues Deutsches Fassungsrecht*, Hirschgraben Verlag. Frankfurt/Main: 1949, pp 15f.

Appendix 15

Full Powers to Ratify the Capitulation

From the Supreme Commander of the Wehrmacht
Headquarters, 7 May 1945

I give powers of plenipotentiary to:

Generalfeldmarschall Keitel as Chief of the OKW and Commander-in-Chief, German Army
Generaladmiral von Friedeburg, Commander-in-Chief, Kriegsmarine
Generaloberst Stumpf, representing Commander-in-Chief, Luftwaffe

To ratify the unconditional surrender of the German armed forces to the Commander-in-Chief Allied Expeditionary Forces and the Soviet High Command.

Dönitz, Grossadmiral.

Source: Extract from *Germany Surrenders Unconditionally, Facsimiles of the Documents*: National Archives Publication 46-4, Washington DC: 1945, p 31.

Appendix 16

Declaration of Capitulation

1. We, the Undersigned, acting with powers of plenipotentiary for and in the name of the High Command of the German Wehrmacht, hereby declare to the Supreme Commander of the Allied Expeditionary Forces and the Commander-in-Chief, Red Army, the unconditional surrender of all

armed forces presently under German command or operated by Germany on land, at sea and in the air.

2. The High Command of the German Wehrmacht will without delay give orders to all commanders of the German land, naval and air forces, and all forces operated by Germany, to cease hostilities at 2301 hrs Central European Time on 8 May and remain in the positions which they occupy at that hour, and to disarm totally by surrendering weapons and equipment to the local Allied commander or officers designated by the Allied representatives. No ship, boat or aircraft of whatever kind may be sunk, nor may be damaged ships' hulls, machinery installations, equipment, machines of all kinds, weapons, apparatus and technical gear which could be of general use for war purposes.

3. The High Command of the German Wehrmacht will pass on without delay to its competent commanders all additional orders received from the Supreme Commander, Allied Expeditionary Forces and the Red Army High Command, and ensure the execution of said orders.

4. This declaration of surrender is made without prejudice to any general capitulation terms being introduced in lieu which may be imposed through the United Nations and in its name on Germany and the German Wehrmacht.

5. In the event that the High Command of the German Wehrmacht or any of the armed forces subordinate to, or controlled by, it should neglect to abide by the terms of this instrument of surrender, the Supreme Commander, Allied Expeditionary Forces and the Red Army High Command will take all such punitive or other measures which they consider appropriate.

This declaration is drawn up in the English, Russian and German languages. The English and Russian versions alone are authentic.

Signed in Berlin, 8 May 1945
Keitel, von Friedeburg, Stumpff for the OKW

In the presence of:
For the Supreme Commander, Allied Expeditionary Forces (illegible)
For the High Commander of the Red Army (illegible)
General, Commanding Colonel of the First French Army (illegible)
Commanding-General, US Strategic Air Forces (Spaatz)

Source: Photo-facsimile of original document (National Archives Publication No 46–4, p 39). The German language version published on 30 April 1946 in the official gazette of the Allied Control Commission for Germany does not correspond with the original document at paras (1) and (4).

Appendix 17

The Grossadmiral OKW/WFSt
Nr 89003/45 G.K.Chefs.
7 May 1945: 12 copies

By telex/signal to: (1) OKM/SKL Admiral Meisel (by courier) (2) OKL to be delivered to Generalmajor Christian (by courier) (3) C-in-C Army Group Kurland, Gen. Der Inf. Hilpert (4) C-in-C Army High Command East Prussia, Gen. Der Panzertruppen von Saucken (5) C-in-C South Generalfeldmarschall Kesselring (6) C-in-C Army Group Centre, Generalfeldmarschall Schörner (7) C-in-C South-east, Generaloberst Löhr (8) C-in-C Ostmark (Austria) Generaloberst Rendulic (9) C-in-C Gebirgs-AOK 20, Gen. Der Gebirgstruppen Böhme (10) Commandant Aegean Generalmajor Wagner (11) Commandant Crete, Generalmajor Benthak (12) To all French enclaves and Channel Islands (13) Inform Führungsgruppe B, Gen der Gebirgstruppen Winter (14) Inform C-in-C North-west, Generalfeldmarschall Busch.

1. On 7 May 1945 0241 hrs total surrender signed by OKW to High Command of the Allied Expeditionary Forces and simultaneously to Soviet High Command for all armed forces on land, sea and in the air.

This was unavoidable to prevent the total destruction of specific sectors of the front expected imminently and thereby to save as many German lives as possible.

2. In accordance therewith all hostilities are to cease on 9 May 1945 0000 hrs German summer time. All command posts of the Army, Kriegsmarine and Luftwaffe, and troops of all Wehrmacht arms of service and Waffen-SS will remain in the positions they occupy at that hour. With immediate effect no naval vessel or aircraft may be sunk or destroyed, no hull, machinery, installation or equipment may be damaged in any way. All further orders which may be issued after 9 May 1945 0000 hrs by the High Command of the Allied Expeditionary Forces and the Soviet High Command are to be carried out. Otherwise the High Command of the Allied Expeditionary Forces and the Soviet High Command will take punitive measures or other steps above and beyond the capitulation conditions.

Supplement for Army Group Kurland and Army High Command East Prussia: All possibilities to ship out by sea before 9 May 1945 0100 hrs are to be pursued using whatever means available. All ships must have sailed before that deadline.

Signed Dönitz, OKW/WFSt Nr 89003/45g.K.Chefs

For the Reich
Signed : Brudermüller, Oberstleutnant, General Staff

12 copies Distribution List: (1) OKM/SKL (2) OKL General Christian (3) Adjustant to Grossadmiral (4) Reich Foreign Minister (5) Chief OKW/WFSt (6) Chief Führungs-Gr./Ktb (7) Chief Ops (Army) (8) Ops (Army) 1a

Source: Militärgeschichtliches Forschungsamt, Freiburg – SKL files. The hour in the Supplement was rectified by an addendum from 0100 to 0000 hrs the same day.

Appendix 18

The Cessation of Hostilities

The OKW has announced:

On 9 May 1945 at 0000 hrs in all theatres of war, all Wehrmacht arms of service, and all armed organisations or individuals will cease hostilities against all former enemies.

Any destruction of or damage to weapons and ammunition, aircraft, armaments, equipment of any kind, including any damage to or sinking of ships, contravenes the conditions accepted and signed for by the OKW in the common interest of the German people and is to be prevented by all means possible. This announcement is to serve as an order for anybody who has not already received the said order through normal channels.

Furthermore with effect from 9 May 1945 0000 hrs signals over all Wehrmacht telegraphic lines are to be sent unciphered.

By order of the Grossadmiral
Signed Jodl, Generaloberst

Source: *Flensburger Nachrichten*, Nr 108, 9 May 1945.

Appendix 19

Broadcast Announcement of Unconditional Surrender by Reichsminister Graf Schwerin von Krosigk, 7 May 1945

'German Men and Women!

By order of Grossadmiral Dönitz, the High Command of the Wehrmacht has today declared the unconditional surrender of all armed forces. As the senior Minister of the Reich Government which the Grossadmiral set up to bring the war to an end, I turn to the German people in this tragic moment of our history. After almost six years of heroic struggle and incomparable hardship, Germany's strength has been sapped by the overwhelming might of our enemies. To have continued the war would have meant senseless blood-shed and useless destruction. A Government with a sense of responsibility for the future of our people had to draw the conclusion from the dwindling away of all physical and material strength and approach the enemy for a cessation of hostilities.

In its last phase, after the fearsome sacrifices which the war has made upon us, it is the primary aim of the Grossadmiral and the Government support-ing him to preserve as many German lives as possible. It was only for this reason that the war could not be stopped immediately and in the West and East simultaneously. In this most difficult hour for the German people and Reich we bow the head in deepest respect before our dead of this war, whose sacrifice is our highest liability.

Our sympathy and concern goes above all to the disabled, the surviving dependants and to all whom this struggle has wounded. Nobody should be in any doubt as to the draconian conditions the enemy will now impose on the German people. It is necessary to brace oneself for it with presence of mind, soberly and without useless rhetoric. Nobody can be in any doubt that the coming times will be harsh for all of us and demand sacrifice of us in all areas of daily life. We have to suffer it and remain true to the liabilities we have inherited. On the other hand we should not despair and silently resign our-selves.

We must allow our way through the darkness to be illuminated by three stars, these being constantly the pledge of our German existence: Unity and Justice and Freedom. From the disintegration of the past we wish to preserve and save one thing: Unity, the concept of a community of one people which found its finest expression in the war, in comradeship at the front, in the neigh-bourly willingness to help out wherever there was need at home. We shall need that comradeship and willingness to help out just as much in the face of the coming famine and poverty as during the fighting and the bombing raids. Only if we can retain Unity and not split apart into quarrelling classes and groups can we get through the hard times ahead.

We must make Justice the principle of our people's life. Justice must be our supreme law and highest guide. Out of inner conviction we must recognise and respect Justice as the foundation of the relationship between peoples. The respect for treaties must be as sacred as the sense that our people belong to the European family of peoples, as whose member we wish to offer all human, moral and material aid to heal the terrible wounds the war has inflicted. Only then can we hope that the tides of hate which today surround Germany throughout the world will recede before the spirit of reconciliation amongst peoples, without which no healing in the world is possible, and that Freedom will again beckon us, that same Freedom without which no people can live a tolerable and dignified existence.

We wish to see our people's future reflected in the innermost and best abilities of the German personality, which have given the world imperishable works and values. We shall combine the heroic struggle of our people with the will, as a member of the western Christian culture, to engage in honest, peaceable work, and make a contribution corresponding to the best traditions of our people.

May God not desert us in our misfortune and bless our difficult task!'

Source: Bundesarchiv Collection R62/10, *Flensburger Nachrichten* No 107, 8 May 1945. ['Unity and Justice and Freedom' – *Einigkeit und Recht und Freiheit* – is the title of the German national anthem. It is the second verse of the original national anthem *Deutschland über alles*. Tr.]

Appendix 20

The Last OKW Report

From the Grossadmiral's HQ, 9 May 1945

'The Oberkommando der Wehrmacht has announced:

In East Prussia, German divisions were still bravely defending to the last yesterday at the Vistula estuary and the western end of the Frische Nehrung.

The 7th Infantry Division distinguished itself particularly. In recognition of the outstanding performance of his troops, its commander-in-chief, General der Panzertruppen von Saucken, has been awarded the Diamonds to his Knight's Cross with Oak-Leaves and Swords.

As the most forward bulwark under their commander-in-chief Generaloberst Hilpert, our armies in Kurland tied down superior forces of Soviet infantry and tanks for months and won immortal fame in six great battles. They rejected all possibility of an early surrender. Only seriously wounded soldiers and fathers with many children were flown out to the West. The Staffs and officers remained with their troops. In accordance with the conditions signed for, at midnight the German side ceased all movement and fighting.

The defenders of Breslau, who held off the Soviets for two months, went under in the final hours after heroic resistance to an enemy superior in numbers and materials. All senior command posts on the South-eastern and Eastern Fronts from Fiume via Brünn to the Elbe at Dresden have received the order to cease hostilities. Czech partisans across nearly all Bohemia and Moravia are threatening the surrender terms and signals communications in the region.

OKW has no fresh reports respecting the situation affecting Army Groups Löhr, Rendulic and Schörner. Far from the Homeland the defenders of the Atlantic enclaves, our troops in Norway and the occupying force in the Aegean islands have preserved the German soldier's military honour by their obedience and discipline.

Since midnight the guns have fallen silent on all fronts. On the orders of the Grossadmiral, the Wehrmacht has abandoned a struggle which had become hopeless. It brings almost six years of heroic fighting to an end. It brought us great victories, but also heavy defeats. The German Wehrmacht has finally lost to a powerful superior force.

True to his oath, the German soldier, with the highest possible commitment to the people, achieved much that will remain unforgotten. The Homeland supported him to the last with all means to hand despite the heaviest sacrifices. The unique achievement of Front and Homeland will find its laudatory appraisal in later impartial reviews. Even the enemy will not fail to pay respect to the achievements and sacrifices of German soldiers on land, water and in the air. Every soldier can therefore stand upright and proud as he puts aside his weapons and in the worst hours for our people goes to work fearless and confident in the eternal life of the nation.

In this dark hour the Wehrmacht remembers its comrades who fell on the fronts. The dead compel us to unconditional loyalty, obedience and discipline to the Fatherland, bleeding from innumerable wounds.'

Source: Text according to file 'OKW 20B', Wehrmacht Command Staff (WFSt), Militärgeschichtliches Forschungsamt der Bundeswehr, Freiburg.

Appendix 21

Last Special Communiqué from Eisenhower's Allied HQ

SHAEF 8 May 1945, 1500 hrs

'All German land, sea and air forces in Europe have surrendered unconditionally to the Allied Expeditionary Forces and the Soviet Russian High Command simultaneously at 0141 hrs Central European Time on 7 May.

The terms of the capitulation, which come into force on 8 May at 2301 hrs Central European Time, were signed by an officer of the German High Command.

The Allied Expeditionary Forces have been instructed to cease hostilities but remain in their present positions until the capitulation takes effect.'

Source: Extract from Keesing's Archiv der Gegenwart, Year 15, Volume 1945.

Appendix 22

Dönitz's Broadcast of 8 May 1945 (transmitted at 1230 hrs on Sender Flensberg)

'German Men and Women!

In my broadcast of 1 May in which I informed the German people of the death of the Führer and my appointment as his successor, I proclaimed it my primary task to save German lives.

To achieve that goal, on the night of 6 May I gave OKW the mission of declaring the unconditional surrender of all our fighting troops in all theatres of war. On 8 May at 2300 hrs the guns will fall silent. The soldiers of the German Wehrmacht, proven in numberless battles, now go down the bitter road to captivity and make the final sacrifice for the lives of our women and children and for the future of our nation. We bow our heads to their bravery proven a thousandfold times and the sacrifice of those who fell and the prisoners.

I have promised the German people that in the coming times of need I shall do the utmost within my power to create tolerable living conditions for our valiant women, men and children. I do not know whether I can make this contribution towards helping you in these harsh times. We have to look the facts in the face. The foundations upon which the German Reich was built have been destroyed. The unity of State and Party no longer exists. The Party has stepped away from the scene of its effectiveness. With Germany occupied, power lies in the hands of the occupying forces. It is up to them whether I, and the Reich Government I have set up, can be active or not. If I can be of use and help to our Fatherland by my activity in office, then I shall remain there either until the will of the peoples of the German Reich finds its expression in the selection of another Head of State, or the occupation authorities make the performance of my office impossible. Only my love for Germany and my duty towards this difficult post keep me here. I shall not remain an hour longer than is compatible with my personal dignity. I owe this to the Reich, whose supreme representative I am.

We all have a difficult road before us. We must proceed down it with dignity, bravery and discipline. Respect for our fallen demands this of us. We must go down it with a will to work, and achieve. Without these we cannot create the basis for a new life for ourselves. We shall go down it accompanied by that Unity and Justice without which we cannot overcome the penury of the days ahead. We shall go down it in the hope that our children will have a free and secure existence in a Europe at peace.

I shall not dally behind you on this thorny road. If you command me to remain in office, then I shall do all I can to help. If you command me to go, I shall consider this step to be equally a service to the people and the Reich.'

Source: *Flensburger Nachrichten*, No 108, 9 May 1945.

Appendix 23

Memorandum Respecting the Caretaker Reich Government

(Handed by Dönitz to the American and British heads of the 'Allied Control Commission at OKW' on 20 May 1945.)

The Caretaker Reich Government was convened by the Grossadmiral in order to effect the task of concluding the war in the area of the civil administration of the Reich. Especially as regards food, trade and industry, transport, and finance for the Reich territory, a string of measures must be taken immediately to avoid a situation developing whose extent and effect cannot be foreseen. These are for the most part matters which cannot be resolved in individual regions but must be handled centrally, for example the distribution of food, coal and other necessities, the circulation of money and foreign exchange, and so on. In the framework of the remaining possibilities, the Caretaker Reich Government is ready to do everything in its power to keep this serious emergency for the German people within reasonable bounds. It believes it can act in the general interest.

The Caretaker Reich Government sees its role as temporary and of limited scope. The time limits are set by the necessity for the German people to express its political will in the constitutional manner, to choose the nature the State will assume, to elect a Head of State and a Reich Government. The statement of this will of the people will not be practical for a period of time beyond the possibility of present assessment. During this period it would seem to be right that the affairs of the Reich Government should be looked after by expert persons especially qualified by experience whose task is transitional and limited to winding up affairs.

For the activity of the Government to be practical, certain preconditions will be necessary:

(a) The heads of the individual administrative branches must have free scope within the German Reich to receive reports from the subordinate authorities and to furnish them with instructions. They must be in a position to be informed personally, or by representatives, regarding the circumstances in the individual regions of the Reich.
(b) They must be able to recruit suitable staff from throughout the Reich as a whole.
(c) Press and radio must be available to them for the dissemination of information to the people, for example in farming, and the issue of instructions to farmers.
(d) The personal organisation of the existing apparatus of administration must be maintained. Certain necessary changes must be withheld until more settled times.
(e) The Government must have the opportunity to transfer its seat to central Germany for better connections to the various corners of the Reich.

Flensburg, 19 May 1945.

Source: Collection R62/3.

Appendix 24

Declaration of the Head of the Allied Control Commission at OKW, Major-General Lowell W. Rooks on the occasion of the arrest of Dönitz, Jodl and von Friedeburg at Flensburg on 23 May 1945

'Gentlemen, I am in receipt of instructions from Supreme Headquarters, European Theatre of Operations, from Supreme Commander, General Eisenhower, to call you before me this morning to tell you that he has decided, in concert with the Soviet High Command, that today the acting German Government and the German High Command, with the several of its members, shall be taken into custody as prisoners of war. Thereby the acting German Government is dissolved. This is now going on. Troops of the 21st Army Group are taking the several members, civilian and military, and certain records, into custody. In conformity with instructions, each of you is to consider yourself a PW from this moment. When you leave this room an Allied officer will attach himself to you and escort you to your quarters where you will pack, have your lunch and complete your affairs, after which they will escort you to the airfield at 1:30 for enplaning. You may take the luggage you require. That's all I have to say.'

Source: *Yank*, Continental Edition of 3 June 1945, 'The Last Act'.

Appendix 25

From: Der Grossadmiral 26 May 1945
To the Commander-in-Chief, 21st British Army Group
Field-Marshal Sir Reginald [*sic*] Montgomery

Dear Field-Marshal!
    I find myself compelled to inform you of the following: After my detention by troops under your command on 23 May at Flensburg, I was obliged to submit to a body search without regard being paid to my rank. At the same

time my private luggage was rummaged. Together with a number of items of value, my marshal's baton was removed. I had placed it in my private luggage deliberately in the belief that this honourable emblem of a soldier of my standing would be respected even by a victorious opponent. I have not received a receipt for the articles of value, nor for the marshal's baton, nor for the interim baton removed from my person during the body search.

As I am sure, Field-Marshal, that any infringement of honour and the inviolability of private property would not be tolerated by yourself, I bring these defamatory incidents to your attention and am convinced that in this manner I shall retrieve the marshal's and interim batons and the private items of property.

I remain,

Yours respectfully
Signed Dönitz.

Source: Draft in possession of the author.

Appendix 26

Extract from the Declaration Considering the Defeat of Germany and the Assumption of Governmental Control with Regard to Germany by the Governments of the United Kingdom, the United States of America, the Union of Soviet Socialist Republics and the Provisional Government of the French Republic

'The German forces on land, sea and in the air have been totally beaten and have surrendered unconditionally. Germany, which is responsible for the war, is no longer capable to resist the will of the victorious Powers. Accordingly the unconditional surrender of Germany has resulted and Germany is now subject to all the demands which will be required of it now or later.

There is in Germany no central Government or authority which would be capable of taking on responsibility for the maintenance of order, for the administration of the country and for the execution of the demands of the victorious Powers.

Under these circumstances it is necessary to prepare for later decisions which may be taken with regard to Germany, precautionary measures to terminate any future hostilities by the German armed forces, to maintain order in Germany, to administer the country and announce the immediate requirements with which Germany is to comply.

The representatives of the Supreme Command authorities of the United Kingdom, the United States of America, the Union of Soviet Socialist Republics and the French Republic, hereinafter called "Allied representatives", which operate with the full authority of their respective Governments and in the interest of the United Nations, issue the following declaration: The Governments of the United Kingdom, the United States or America, the Union of Soviet Socialist Republics and the provisional Government of the French Republic hereby take over the national Government of Germany, including all functions of the German Government, of the Supreme Command of the Wehrmacht, administrations or authorities of the regions, cities and municipalities. The assumption of the aforementioned power of Government and functions for the purposes stated will not bring about the annexation of Germany.'

Source: Official Gazette of the Control Council for Germany, 30 April 1946. The declaration, which goes on to list the individual demands of the 'Allied representatives', with whom 'all German authorities and the German people are obliged to comply unconditionally' under threat of punitive measures, was signed in the three operative languages (English, French and Russian) by Eisenhower, Montgomery, Zhukov and de Lattre-Tassigny on 5 June 1945 in Berlin, and came into effect the same day.

Appendix 27

A Statement by the Governments of the UK, USA and USSR, and the Provisional Government of France respecting the zones of occupation in Germany

'1. For the purposes of occupation within its frontiers as they existed at 31 December 1937, Germany is to be divided into four zones, of which each of the Four Powers will occupy one zone as follows:

- an Eastern Zone for the USSR
- a North-western Zone for the United Kingdom
- a South-western Zone for the United States of America
- a Western Zone for France

The occupation troops in each Zone will be under the control of a Commander-in-Chief appointed by the responsible Power. Each of the four Powers may if so required incorporate into the body of the occupation troops under the command of its commander-in-chief auxiliary units from the armed forces of any other Allied Power which was actively involved in military operations against Germany, the area of Greater Berlin will be occupied by troops from each of the Four Powers. For the purpose of the common administrative control of this area, an inter-Allied authority (Russian=Kommendatura) will be set up with four commandants each nominated by the respective commander-in-chiefs.'

5 June 1945

Source: Official Gazette of the Control Council for Germany, 30 April 1946.

Appendix 28

By: Grossadmiral Dönitz, Bad Mondorf, July 1945.

'On 7 July the commandant of the camp in which I am being held as a prisoner-of-war read out an instruction consisting of three paragraphs. Amongst other matters paragraph 2 contained the statement that '... the German *State* has ceased to exist'. Following my objection, the sentence was amended to read '... the German *Government* has ceased to exist'.

In order to avoid misunderstandings of my personal position, I would like to make the following clarification:

(1) The capitulation was concluded by my plenipotentiaries on the basis of written powers which I supplied in my role as Head of State of the German Reich and Supreme Commander of the Wehrmacht, and which in this form had been required and recognised by the plenipotentiaries of the Allied armed forces. By this procedure the Allies recognise me as Head of State of the German Reich.

(2) The agreed unconditional surrender of the three Wehrmacht arms of service, signed by my authority on 9 May 1945, neither brought an end to the existence of the German Reich nor to my office as Head of State. Furthermore the Caretaker Government formed by me remains in office: the Allied Monitoring Commission at Flensburg continued business dealings with it until 23 May.

(3) In connection with the capitulation, the subsequent total occupation of the area of the German Reich changed nothing as regards *the situation in law*. All it has done is prevent myself and my Government from governing Germany.

(4) Equally, taking my Government and my person prisoner has no effect on the explained situation in law. The only consequence of the sequestration has been that all actual official activity for myself and my Government has ceased completely.

(5) Having stated this opinion as regards the legal effects of the mentioned military proceedings, I declare myself in agreement with the generally accepted principles of international law.'

Signed, Dönitz

Source: Draft in German and English with hand-written corrections by Dönitz in author's possession.

Notes

Foreword
1. Admiral zur besonderen Verwendung – 'Admiral for Special Purposes'.

Section I: The Dönitz Government – The Last Days of the Third Reich

Chapter 1: Autumn 1944 to April 1945: Impressions at Führer-Headquarters

1. The statistics vary depending on whether one accepts the production figures supplied by industry or the Luftwaffe. The production of day fighters ordered by the Wehrmacht for 1942 was reportedly 4,476, for 1943 9,121, for 1944 20,242. The 1944 output trailed 30 per cent behind the production plan due to air raids against production centres and transport, despite the full availability of raw materials and labour. That in the year of bombing terror 1944 almost five times the number of fighters were built than in 1942, when no serious disruption to production occurred, shows two things with equal clarity: (a) the total misjudgment by the leadership from the outbreak of war as to how the military situation would develop, and (b) the lack of preparation of German industry for the war. In the opinion of Speer, the last Minister for Armaments, organisation and central planning were co-ordinated far too late to meet wartime requirements.
2. On 13 May 1945 in the House of Commons, Churchill compared the U-boat threat faced at the end of the war to that of 1942, the most successful year for the U-boats. The extraordinary interest after the capitulation in the recruitment of German armaments specialists (particularly in V-weapons and aircraft production) by the various victor states proves that at the end of the war Germany led the world in its technological developments in many fields which, however, it had become impossible for Germany to use herself.

3. The development of the jet fighter was obstructed in the first instance by Göring's lack of interest in it. In 1943 Hitler ordered it to be forced through. Unfavourable factors in the summer of 1944 held back its operational readiness. Hitler then discarded his last trump card, contrary to the urgings of OKW, the Luftwaffe and the Armaments Ministry, by ordering that the jet fighter should be produced as a fighter-bomber. In the opinion of the technical experts this delayed the introduction of these aircraft by at least six, if not twelve months. Discussion about this Führer-order became so prevalent at HQ, and so bitter in nature, that Hitler soon intervened and forbade any further talk on the subject.

4. Two reserve divisions facing the correctly identified enemy assembly point did not receive their operational orders in time and were overrun by the Russian flood when it broke through. Hitler ordered Generaloberst Harpe, Commander-in-Chief, Army Group Centre, relieved of his command immediately. I happened to be in the anteroom of the Führer's chamber when Harpe arrived to deliver his report. I was surprised at how calm and sure-footed he was. He placed before Hitler a 'Führer-order' sent to him by telex on the basis of which Harpe had not moved his two divisions. This order, whose existence was unknown to Hitler, had been issued by the Army General Staff, which ran operations in the East. There had apparently been an error, not a 'betrayal'. German forces on the Eastern Front, weakened by the diversion of men and material to the Ardennes, were outnumbered 7:1 and ultimately the collapse was hardly avoidable.

5. I consider it probable that well into late April 1945 Hitler was consumed by faith in Providence. Only this can explain his spontaneous reaction to the news of Roosevelt's death when, contrary to his custom, he phoned Dönitz in great excitement to inform him personally of the glad tidings. Dönitz received the report with the sober observation that in his opinion a favourable political result for Germany was not to be expected for the time being.

Chapter 2: Dönitz Leaves Berlin

1. This copy I meanwhile placed at the disposal of the historian Percy E. Schramm, who published it verbatim in his book *Die Niederlage 1945*, Munich: DTV-Dokumente, 1962.

Chapter 6: The Military Situation on 2 May 1945

1. Loss of Antwerp, September 1944. All supplies for Montgomery's Army Group came through the intact port at Antwerp. The desperate but

unsuccessful attempts by the Germans to put it out of action by the use of V-weapons and special operations by the Kriegsmarine and Luftwaffe, and so cut the Thames-Scheldt traffic, failed because of the distance involved.

Loss of the Rhine bridge at Remagen. After the event a vain attempt was made to destroy the bridge using Kriegsmarine frogmen led by the Knights' Cross holder Korvettenkapitän Bartels,. The main bridge was collapsed by two remote-guided V-2 rockets [NB: author states 'aircraft' incorrectly. Tr.], but by then the enemy had already established a bridgehead on the opposite bank and constructed an additional auxiliary bridge.

Chapter 7: Realisation and Decision

1. [With the exception of the negotiations on 1 May 1945 for the surrender of Berlin initiated by Bormann which were rejected by the Russians because it was not a total capitulation to all Allies simultaneously. Tr.]

2. The oath of the German soldier laid down by the law of 20 August 1934 was: 'Ich schwöre bei Gott diesen heiligen Eid, dass ich dem Führer des deutschen Reiches und Volkes Adolf Hitler, dem Oberbefehlshaber der Wehrmacht, unbedingt Gehorsam leisten und als tapferer Soldat bereit sein willm jederzeit für diesen Eid mein Leben einzusetzen'. ('I swear by God this holy oath, that I will give the Führer of the German Reich and People, Adolf Hitler, the Supreme Commander-in-Chief of the Wehrmacht, unconditional obedience and will be prepared as a brave soldier to risk my life at any time for this oath'. The oath of the Waffen-SS soldier was: 'Ich schwöre Dir, Adolf Hitler, als Führer und Kanzler des Reiches, Treue und Tapferkeit. Ich gelobe Dir und den von Dir bestimmten Vorgesetzten Gehorsam bis in den Tod. So wahr mir Gott helfe.' ('I swear to thee, Adolf Hitler, as Führer and Chancellor of the Reich, loyalty and bravery. I pledge to thee and those thou set above me obedience unto death. So help me God.')

3. The relevant section of the order of the day for the Wehrmacht of 1 May 1945 can be seen at Appendix 7b, paragraph beginning 'The situation demands of you ...' to the end.

Chapter 8: Partial Capitulation in the North

1. Feldmarschall Busch, to my knowledge considered honourable even by the enemy, and whose area of command was the venue for this capitulation, spoke with great indignation later about this 'dishonourable' ceremony. In contrast to the much younger and more adaptable von Friedeburg, he never forgave the British for this lack of chivalry.

Chapter 9: Unconditional Surrender

1. Despite the disaster of the passenger ship *Wilhelm Gustloff*, the losses T SEA from the autumn of 1944 of persons being evacuated to the Western Baltic were below 1 per cent. These were therefore substantially lower that the figures for the long treks on land where hunger, cold and enemy action all had serious effects.

Chapter 11: The Unpolitical Cabinet

1. On Dönitz's instructions, on 3 May Reich Minister Speer made a radio broadcast concerning the near future in which he saw the most important tasks as being the restoration of the roads and agricultural production.

Chapter 13: Abdication?

1. Article 51 of the Weimar Constitution (*Reichsgesetzblatt* 1932, Part I, p 547) stated: 'In the case of his disability, the Reich President will be represented by the President of the Reich Court. The same applies to the case of a premature disposal of the Presidency until the conclusion of a fresh General Election.'

Chapter 14: East or West?

1. On 9 May at the Mürwik naval college, Dönitz delivered a final address to the officer corps of all Wehrmacht arms gathered at Flensburg. An account of events, the alignment to the West and preservation of dignity and discipline were the main points of his speech. A second speech scheduled for eight days later aboard an escort ship for the officers of the S-boat Arm was cancelled because Schwerin von Krosigk advised him against leaving the 'enclave'.

Chapter 16: The Arrest of the Caretaker Reich Government

1. In contrast to this, at Nuremberg in its judgment of Grossadmiral Dönitz (afternoon session, 1 October 1946) the IMT declared: 'On 1 May 1945 he became Hitler's successor as Head of State.'

Section II: The Dönitz Government in Modern Academic Research

Chapter 1: The Struggle for the Succession

1. H. R. Trevor-Roper, *Hitlers Letzte Tage*, Zürich: 1948, p 23.
2. IMT Vol IX, p 344. During the annexation when Hitler was in Austria, Göring acted as his deputy: IMT Vol IX p 336. Apparently Hitler preferred Göring to Hess because the latter had no feeling for art and culture: Otto Dietrich, *12 Jahre mit Hitler*, Munich: 1955, p 204.
3. *Der grossdeutsche Freiheitskampf* (Adolf Hitler's speeches, 1 September 1939–10 March 1940), Munich 1940, p 26 (see Appendix 1).
4. Karl Koller, *Der letzte Monat* (diary notes of the former Chief of the Luftwaffe General Staff, 14 April 1945–27 May 1945) Mannheim: 1945, p 37.
5. Statement by Bodenschatz: IMT Vol IX pp 16f, 38f, 41. Also see Goebbels, *Diaries, 1942–1943*, publ. Louis P. Lochner, Zürich: 1948, pp 254f, 257 (9 March 1943): for the attempt to 'activate' Göring, pp 238ff (2 March 1943).
6. War Diary OKW (Wehrmacht Command Staff) with introduction and commentary by Percy Ernst Schramm, Frankfurt/Main 1961, Vol 4, 2.Half-Vol, p 1781, Note 1. [**Transl. Note:** Note however that Felix Kersten quoted Himmler as knowing about this electoral college as early as 20 October 1942 in Rome: 'Himmler explained that after the war a senate would elect the new Führer. It would be made up of all the Gauleiters, ten of the Party heads, ten of the principal SS leaders, five SA leaders and one Reichs-Minister. The Führer's successor would be elected from amongst these men. It was the best system a Herrenvolk could have to elect the Führer. Afterwards the senate would take on other missions and have a permanent role.' Kersten, Felix, *Yo fuí confidente de Himmler*, Barcelona: 1967, p 331 *Possible Election of New Führer in Enclave*.]
7. For Hitler's ideas see his speech, 1 September 1939, *ibid*, p 26 (Note 3), and H Heims, *Hitlers Tischgespräche im FHQ 1941-1942*, publ. Schramm (amongst others), Stuttgart: 1963, pp 234ff, esp p 236 and p 411ff.
8. Koller (Note 4), pp 11ff, 14–16.
9. Dietrich (Note 2), p 256; Albert Zoller, *Hitler privat*, Düsseldorf: 1949, p 13.
10. Keitel, 'The Last Days in Berlin', in *Nazi Conspiracy and Aggression*, Supplement B, Washington DC: 1948, pp 1284ff; Dietrich (Note 2), p 262.
11. Werner Bross, *Gespräche mit Hermann Göring*, Flensburg/Hamburg: 1950, p 187.

12. For a well-substantiated attempt to bring Göring to account see Walter Baum, 'Der Zusammenbruch der obersten deutschen militärischen Führung' in *Wehrwissenschaftliche Rundschau*, Year 1960, p 247, note 13.

13. Trevor Roper (Note 1), p 91 fn 8.

14. Zoller (Note 9), pp 204f.

15. Koller (Note 4), p 31; Keitel (Note 10), p 1277; Walter Görlitz, *Generalfeldmarschall Keitel, Verbrecher oder Offizier?*, Göttingen: 1961, p 347; Trevor Roper (Note 1), p 116 note 2 and p 131; Hildegard Springer, *Es sprach Hans Fritzsche, Nach Gesprächen, Briefen, Dokumenten*, Stuttgart: 1949, p 48.

16. Springer (Note 15), p 40.

17. Baum (Note 12), p 247 note 15.

18. Koller (Note 4), p 37 et seq.

19. Koller (Note 4), pp 38f, information from KAdm (ret'd) von Puttkamer to the author.

20. Koller (Note 4), pp 38f, Trevor Roper (Note 1), p 124; KTB/OKW (Note 6), p 1456.

21. Koller (Note 4), p 95; Trevor Roper (Note 1), p 131 and p 142.

22. Hans Baur, *Ich flog Mächtige der Erde*, Kempten: 1956, p 268.

23. See Speer's narrative, although this seems somewhat exaggerated: G. M. Gilbert, *Nürnberger Tagebuch*, Frankfurt/Main; 1962, p 198; to the contrary Bross (Note 11), pp 253, 227 and 183f.

24. Keitel (Note 10), pp 1284ff.

25. Trevor-Roper (Note 1), pp 131f; Koller (Note 4), p 70; Baur (Note 22), p 269.

26. Joachim Schultz, *Die letzten 30 Tage*, Stuttgart: 1951, pp 40f. *Flensburger Nachrichten*, edition of 27 April 1945.

27. Baum (Note 12), p 248 note 21; Bross (Note 11), p 228; Gilbert (Note 23), pp 205f.

28. Baur (Note 22), p 269.

29. Koller (Note 4), pp 41ff.

30. Koller (Note 4), pp 43 and 88.

31. Information from KAdm von Puttkamer to the author also *et seq*.

32. Koller (Note 4), pp 42ff, 73ff.

33. Koller (Note 4), pp 75ff, 79ff.

34. Oberst von Brauchitsch, Göring's adjutant, saw all these events in a more kindly light according to his testimony at Nuremberg: IMT Vol IX, pp 164f.

35. See Appendix 3.

36. Koller (Note 4), p 79.

37. Assumptions in naval circles, information to author.
38. A parallel case to Bormann's hate-filled offensive against Göring was his attempt to have Generaloberst Heinrici tried for high treason: IfZ, Munich, ZS66.
39. Koller (Note 4), p 88.
40. Koller (Note 4) p 80.
41. Koller (Note 4), p 88; IMT Vol IX pp 480f.
42. Koller (Note 4), pp 88, 91. Michael A. Musmanno, *In zehn Tagen kommet der Tod*, Munich: 1951, p 103f; Gilbert (Note 23), p 186.
43. According to a man of the German 'resistance', it would appear that the Western Powers were inclined for some time to negotiate with Göring if itler were deposed: recollection of author.
44. Bross (Note 11), p 213. The Americans treated him with such open friendliness that the British and American public complained: Joe H Heydecker and Johannes Leeb, *Der Nürnberger Prozess*, Cologne-Berlin 1958, pp 17ff; Koller (Note 4), pp 91, 98f – for Göring's fantasy in captivity see *Keesings Archiv der Gegenwart*, Vol 15/1945, pp 221f.
45. Heydecker and Leeb (Note 44), pp 23f.
46. Generalmajor Dethleffsen's notes from the winter of 1945/46, which he kindly allowed the author to inspect; Schwerin von Krosigk, interrogation ZS 145 Vol 1 (IfZ Archiv, Munich).
47. Karl O. Paetel, *Die SS – A Contribution to the Sociology of National Socialism*, VfZG Vol 2/1954 pp 12f; also the statements of Körner, IMT Vol IX, p 176, Milch, *ibid*, p 61, Brauchitsch, *ibid*, p 169, Göring, *ibid*, p 676, also Serge Lang and Ernst von Schenck, *Portrait eines Menschheitsverbrechers*, based on memoirs of former Reich Minister Alfred Rosenberg, St Gallen: 1947, pp 204f, 290.
48. Lutz Graf Schwerin von Krosigk, unpublished diary, entries 28 and 29 April 1945 (IfZ Archiv Munich).
49. Lang and Schenck (Note 47), p 290; Zoller (Note 9), pp 204f.
50. Siegfried Westphal, *Heer in Fesseln* (from the papers of Chief of Staff of Rommel, Kesselring and Rundstedt), Bonn: 1950, pp 285ff.
51. Heinz Guderian, *Erinnerungen eines Soldaten*, Heidelberg: 1951, pp 366ff, 375ff, 383f.
52. Zoller (Note 9), p 208 and Stuckart: Schwerin (Note 48), diary entry 28 April 1945, both allege tension between Hitler and Himmler.
53. Schellenberg: *Nazi Conspiracy and Aggression*, Supplement B, Washington DC, 1948, p 1632; also his *Memoiren*, Cologne: 1959, pp 357ff, 366; Schwerin, interrogation (Unpublished IfZ Munich).

54. Karl Dönitz, original text of the relevant section of his memoirs in *Quick* magazine, No 19/1958 p 44f; it had been removed from the book when it appeared later. The correct date was 27 April, as can be determined from the draft for the 'White Book' of Gauleiter Wegener: unpubl. Bundesarchiv Koblenz, collection R62. See also Görlitz (Note 15), p 359 with note 43.

55. Musmanno (Note 42), p 368; Schwerin von Krosigk, 'Die bedingungslose Kapitulation' in *Christ und Welt* No 17/1955 p 16 and also his diary entry 22 April 1945 (Note 48).

56. Schwerin von Krosigk, diary entry 28 and 29 April 1945 (Note 48).

57. Karl Dönitz, *Zehn Jahre und zwanzig Tage*, Bonn: 1958, p 439.

58. For general treatment see: Count Folke Bernadotte, *Das Ende – Meine Handlungen in Deutschland im Frühjahr 1945 und ihre politische Folgen*, Zürich, New York: 1945; Harry S. Truman, *Memoiren*, Vol 1 (1945), Stuttgart: 1955, pp 124ff, also Gerhard Ritter, *Carl Goerdeler und die Widerstandsbewegung*, 3rd edition, Stuttgart: 1956, pp 427ff.

59. OKW War Diary (Note 6), p 1463.

60. Copy of statement dated 29 April 1945, SKL files (unpublished); Dönitz (Note 57), pp 440f; OKW War Diary p 146.

61. Dönitz (Note 57), pp 440f.

62. Dönitz, letter to author, 8 December 1962.

63. Dönitz explains his conduct as being the result of a lack of real means of power against Himmler and the fear of internal strife (Note 57), pp 440, 443, 468; letter of 28 January 1961 to the author. In fact he had the possibilities which the Führer-order of 20 April 1945 gave him (SKL files: 1 SKL.B No. 864/45, Chefsache 21.4.1945: see Appendix 2. In this case he had not taken advantage of it, but entered the 'lion's den' with a small escort, where Himmler could easily have overpowered him: see pp 42f.

64. Dönitz (Note 57), pp 308f.

65. Dönitz (Note 57), pp 307f; also written replies to questions at Nuremberg prison unpubl. Folio 4f (private collection).

66. Dönitz (Note 57), pp 308f. Regarding the war at sea in general: Friedrich Ruge, *Der Seekrieg 1939-1945* Stuttgart: 1954; Kurt Assmann, *Deutsche Seestrategie in zwei Weltkriegen*, Heidelberg: 1957; also Jürgen Rohwer, 'Der U-bootkreig und sein Zusammenbruch 1943' in *Entscheidungsschlachten des Zweiten Weltkrieges*, Frankfurt/Main: 1960, pp 327ff, and Walter Baum, 'Der Zweite Weltkrieg' in *Neue Politische Literatur*, 7.Year 1962, pp 258ff.

67. Dönitz, *Rede auf der Gauleitertagung in Posen*, 6 October 1943, unpubl. Extract from *Keesings Archiv der Gegenwart*, 8.10.1943, p 6129B; mentioned briefly in

Brassey's Naval Annual 1948, London-New York; secret telex of 31 January 1945 (unpubl,) and memorandum of 28 February 1945 (unpubl. SKL files).

68. See e.g. the 'special situation' of 11 April 1945: IMT Vol XXXV, pp 304ff.
69. For Hitler's Testament re Kriegsmarine, see Appendix 3. For the attitude of the Kriegsmarine see Walter Baum, *Marine, Nationalsozialismus und Widerstand* in: VfZG 11/1963, pp 16ff, also publ. in the supplement to weekly *Das Parlament*: from *Politik in Zeitgeschichte*, No. B29/63, 17 July 1963, pp 17ff.
70. Hitler's Testament, Appendix 3; Dönitz (Note 57) pp 442; Karl Jesko von Puttkamer, *Die unheimliche See, Hitler und die Kriegsmarine*, Vienna-Munich: 1952, p 63.
71. Dönitz (Note 57), p 441; Musmanno (Note 42), p 358.
72. The last Chief of the Army General Staff General Krebs made such indications in mid-April: Dethleffsen (Note 46), folio 57.
73. See above, p 41 – One the other hand neither Admiral Meisel, SKL head, KAdm Godt, head of 2/SKL BdU Op nor Kriegsmarine liaison officer at FHQ VizeAdm Voss knew or suspected anything of an imminent appointment of Dönitz; communications to the author; Dönitz, letter of 28 Jan 1961 to author. More junior officers at SKL considered the nomination certain; letters to the author, also Puttkamer (Note 70), p 63. Schwerin von Krosigk considered that if he did it at all, Hitler would appoint a serving officer, either Kesselring or Dönitz, who were the respective heads of 'Southern' and 'Northern' parts of Germany respectively; Schwerin von Krosigk, interrogation (unpubl. Archiv der IfZ Munich). Also see signal of 29 Apr 1945 sent 2307 hrs from Puttkamer to Dönitz, that OKW South considered his appointment necessary when the Reich fell (unpubl. Bundesarchiv Koblenz, collection R62). Dönitz himself is convinced that his appointment can be traced back to the urgings of Speer; Dönitz (Note 57) p 442 and letters to author, 28 January 1962 and 8 December 1962. This idea is very doubtful, at that time Speer did not have the same welcome at FHQ as formerly and had lost influence (ZS 66/I p 89, 103 Archiv IfZ Munich). Moreover it is very odd that he did not convey this to Dönitz until much later while informing Schwerin von Krosigk straight away. Schwerin von Krosigk said that he had proposed Dönitz: diary entry 1 May 1945 (unpubl. p 48). Dönitz knew no other details, letter of 8 December 1962 to the author. Possibly both were fantasies.
74. Dönitz (Note 57), p 440; Schwerin von Krosigk diary entry, 30 April 1945 (Note 48).

75. General Winter (OKW South) wrote asking Jodl on 20 April for a forecast of the succession: OKW War Diary (Note 6), p 1466.

76. Dönitz (Note 57), pp 441, 444, 452; for the signals see OKW War Diary (Note 6), pp 1468f, also *Die Niederlage* 1945. From the OKW War Diary, version publ. by Percy Ernst Schramm, 1962, pp 419f. Also see Appendix 5.

77. OKW War Diary (Note 6), p 1468; *Die Niederlage* (Note 76), p 419.

78. Speer was decisive here: draft of signal (unpubl.), Bundesarchiv Koblenz (collection R62/2).

79. Correspondence with author.

80. Trevor-Roper (Note 1), p 193; Musmanno (Note 42), pp 359f; Baur (Note 22), p 279; Helmut Weidling, 'Der Endkampf in Berlin (23 April–2 May 1945)' in *Wehrwissenschftliche Rundschau* Year 12/1962, pp 170ff; therefore the Soviet High Command knew of Hitler's suicide and the contents of his Testament; Weidling p 171, see also Joseph Wulf, *Martin Bormann – Hitlers Schatten*, Gütersloh: 1962, pp 229f.

81. Baur (Note 22), p 287; Springer (Note 15), p 55.

82. Dönitz (Note 57), p 453; Schwerin von Krosigk, letter to author, 7 December 1962.

83. See his speech of 1 May 1945, Appendix 7a. The pictures of the Führer in the service quarters were not removed until 14 May 1945 at Allied insistence; Dönitz diary, entry 14 May 1945 in *Die Niederlage* (Note 76), p 445. OKW War Diary (Note 6), p 1498; Dönitz, *Fragebogen* (questionmark) in Nuremberg Prison (unpubl). The NSDAP, which Rosenberg had not been able to disband in the face of the objections of the 'Old Party members' was finally terminated on 8 May at Schwerin von Krosigk's suggestion after a remark made by Dönitz in a speech that day (Appendix 22); Schwerin; *Fragebogen* (unpubl, Archiv IfZ Munich), *Flensburger Nachrichten*, 9 May 1945.

84. Dönitz was immediately agreeable to Schwerin's suggestion to arrest Goebbels and Bormann: Schwerin, letter to author, 7 December 1962.

85. Note the strange remark by Jodl at the situation conferences (12–20 May 1945) in OKW War Diary (Note 6), pp 1499ff.

Chapter 2: Making the Dönitz Government

1. Dönitz (Note 57), pp 446, 452, Appendix 3a.

2. Respecting a statement by Hitler shortly after Hindenburg's death (1934) that he would perhaps un-merge the offices of Reich President and Reich Chancellor one day, see Otto Meissner, *Staatssekretär unter Ebert-Hindenburg-Hitler*, Hamburg: 1950, p 388.

3. Dönitz, letter 8 December 1962 to author.
4. See also Dönitz (Note 57), pp 452f.
5. Dönitz diary, 2 May 1945 (Note 83), pp 421f.
6. Schwerin, 'Kapitulation' in *Christ und Welt*, No 15/1955, p 8, also interrogation, unpubl. Archiv Ifz Munich; Keitel, *Erinnerungen* (Note 15), p 372.
7. Dönitz diary 2 May 1945 (Note 83), p 422. See also the clash between General Weidling, last military defender of Berlin, and Goebbels, 30 April 1945: upon hearing of the terms of Hitler's Testament he enquired, 'Herr Reich Minister, do you seriously believe that the Russians would negotiate with a German Government in which you are the Reich Chancellor?' – Weidling (Note 80), p 171.
8. Dönitz diary, 2 May 1945 (Note 83), p 422.
9. Schwerin von Krosigk, *Es geschah in Deutschland*, Tübingen and Stuttgart: 1951, p 239.
10. Schwerin (Note 48), diary entry 1 May 1945, also 'Kapitulation' (Note 55), No 15, p 8; Dönitz, letter 8 December 1962; for the alleged role of Speer see Note 73.
11. Albert Vögler was a Ruhr industrialist (for general coverage see Gert von Klass, *Albert Vögler*, Tübingen: 1957. Hermann Bücher was chairman of AEG, Karl Lindemann from Bremen was proprietor of the China firm Melchers and for years president of the International Chamber of Commerce: Münchmeyer was a major Hamburg businessman. Schwerin, diary entry 1 May 1945, and letter to author of 7 December 1962, et seq.
12. Note 95 and Schwerin (Note 94), p 357; Dönitz (Note 57), pp 446f.
13. Letter from KKpt (ret'd) Lüdde-Neurath to the author from his notes.
14. Dönitz, *Quick* No 20/1958 (Note 54), p 72; in a somewhat modified form (Note 57), p 477; Schwerin (Note 94), p 374 and letter to author 28 December 1962. Keitel applied for discharge from office on his own account: Görlitz (Note 15), p 372.
15. Initially Dönitz also considered relieving Jodl of his post because of his lack of experience at the front: Note 99.
16. If Manstein had replaced Keitel, Jodl would also have gone on the basis of his declaration of solidarity with Keitel: Schwerin (Note 94), p 374.
17. Advice kindly provided by KAdm Godt to the author.
18. According to Jodl, Dönitz was glad not to have cast Keitel adrift at this time: Jodl, diary, 13 May 1945 (microfilm copy, IfZ Archive Munich).
19. OKW War Diary (Note 6), pp 1463ff; Dönitz diary (Note 83) entry 13 May 1945, p 444; Görlitz (Note 15), pp 379f; Jodl, diary (Note 103).

20. Notes, Dethleffsen (Note 46), folio 62f; Dönitz diary (Note 83) entry 2 May and 3 May 1945, pp 422, 424; also Schultz (Note 26), p 72, OKW War Diary (Note 6), p 1473.
21. The word 'enclave' was thrown into the discussions by Generalmajor Dethleffsen and adopted officially.
22. Notes of Adm (ret'd) Bürkner (ZS No 364 IfZ Archive Munich).
23. Schwerin, 'Kapitulation' (Note 55) No 18, p 16; radio speeches by Dönitz 1 May 1945, Speer 3 May 1945, Schwerin 2 May and 7 May, and Dönitz 8 May; *Flensburger Nachrichten* of following day; Schwerin, 'Kapitulation' (Note 55) No 15, p 8 and letter to author, 28 December 1962; telegram 6 May 1945 to German Embassy, Tokyo, IMT document NG-4685; for several overseas cables sent and received see collection R/62, Bundesarchiv Koblenz (unpubl).
24. OKW War Diary (Note 6), pp 1496, 1947.
25. See Speer's statement on his arrest: 'Now the end has come. It is best. It was all a kind of opera beforehand.' Heydecker and Leeb (Note 44), p 35; also Dönitz diary, entry 10 May 1945 (Note 83), pp 437f; the Nazi war flag was not taken down until 10 May when insisted upon by CO, British 11th Armoured Division; finally see Jodl's notable opinions at the situation conferences, OKW War Diary (Note 6), pp 1499f.
26. Eisenhower's proclamation in autumn 1944 when the Allies reached German soil: Official Circular of the Military Government of Germany, Control Area, 21 Army Group No 2, p 1; also publ. by Rolf Stödter, *Deutschlands Rechtslage*, Hamburg: 1948, pp 15f. As regards the early history of the later Nuremberg Trials from the Allied side see Telford Taylor, *Die Nürnberger Prozesse, Kriegsverbrechen und Völkerrecht*, Zürich: 1951.
27. From 11 May the word 'armistice' was replaced by 'capitulation': OKW War Diary (Note 6), p 1491. For Montgomery's attitude towards GFM Busch: Field Marshal Montgomery: *Memoirs*, Fontana, Glasgow: 1960, pp 375f. General Fangohr, head of the German liaison staff to Eisenhower was told by Eisenhower's Chief of Operations Section: 'Your status and that of your liaison staff is that of prisoners of war'. OKW War Diary (Note 6), p 1499.
28. Drew Middleton, 'German Government Ended' in *New York Times*, 24 May 1945: Heydecker-Leeb (Note 44), pp 32ff. Later Churchill disapproved of the manner in which the arrests had been made in a letter dated 5 June 1945 to Montgomery: Winston S Churchill, *Der Zweite Weltkrieg*, Vol 6 Book 2, Stuttgart: 1954, p 422.

Chapter 3: The Capitulation
1. Sonderlage, 11 April 1945: IMT Vol XXXV pp 304ff; Schwerin, diary 25 April 1945 (Note 48).
2. Unpubl. Diary, KAdm Godt, entry 30 April 1945, et seq. Actually the 'change' had come about shortly before. Whereas Dönitz had been originally disposed to defend the North with all means at his command, according to Hitler's orders, his attitude was finally changed under the pressure of circumstances; see his telex to Gauleiter Kaufmann 30 April 1945 which he sent before receiving news of the change in succession (Appendix 4).
3. Hitler's order of 19 March 1945 for a scorched earth policy and Speer's objections in his letter to Hitler of 29 March, see *Niederlage 1945* (Note 76), p 407ff.
4. Dönitz diary, 2 May 1945 (Note 83) p 421.
5. Generaloberst Lindemann was even determined to begin 'the last decent battle of the war' with his still intact force: Schwerin, *Es geschah* (Note 94), p 370; also 'Kapitulation' (Note 55) No 16, p 16; also personal reports from a participant at the conference of 3 May 1945 (Dönitz diary [Note 83], p 424). On the other hand Lindemann and GFM Busch made known on 30 April through an envoy in Stockholm that they would be prepared to surrender if the Allies reached Lübeck. The reason for this condition was their fear of Waffen-SS troops, who would not be cut off until then. Eisenhower, *Crusade in Europe*, Perma Books, Garden City, New York 1952, p 469.
6. Schwerin: affidavit of 30 April 1949 (Archiv IfZ Munich); Dönitz diary, 2 May 1945 (Note 83), pp 421 et seq.
7. Schwerin, 'Kapitulation' (Note 55) No 15, p 8.
8. Also see Anne Armstrong, *Unconditional Surrender*, New Brunswick, New Jersey: 1961; Alfred Vogts, 'Unconditional Surrender – Before and After 1945' in VfZG 7/1959, p 280ff; Günter Mottmann, 'Die Genesis der Unconditional Surrender Forderung', in *Wehrwissenschaftliche Rundschau* 8/1956, pp 105ff, 177ff.
9. Dönitz (Note 57), p 442.
10. Schwerin, 'Kapitulation' (Note 55) No 15, p 8; also *Es geschah* (Note 94), p 368f. Letters from Schwerin modify his statements here.
11. OKW War Diary 10 April 1945 (Note 6), pp 1233 and 1494, fn1, p 1504, fn2.
12. Theodor Schieder (English translation) *The Expulsion of German Populations from the Territories East of the Oder-Neisse* (publ. Fed.Min. for Expelled Persons) Vol I/1, 1953, Introduction p 60ff.

13. Dönitz diary, entry 2 May 1945 (Note 83), p 421; proclamation 1 May 1945 Appendix 7a. Schwerin, 'Kapitulation' (Note 55) No 15, p 8, also *Es geschah* (Note 94), pp 368f.

14. Contrary to an earlier impression (Baum [Note 12], p 264), after further investigation it is confirmed that Hitler and his fanatical follower GFM Schörner were responsible: kind information of General Foertsch, from 25 April 1945 Chief of Army General Staff, Army Group Kurland (letter to author 3 December 1962).

15. The achievement of the Kriegsmarine was magnificent: between 23 January and 8 May 1945 sea transports carried 2,022,602 persons to safety from the East: situation report I Ost 521/45, 22 May 1945 (SKL files), also Dönitz (Note 57), p 465.

16. Schwerin, 'Kapitulation' (Note 55) No 15, p 8: No 16, p 16; Dönitz diary entry 2 May 1945 (Note 83), p 422.

17. Dönitz (Note 57), p 465.

18. Schwerin, 'Kapitulation' (Note 55) No 16, p 16; Schwerin, *Es geschah* (Note 94), p 369; Dönitz (Note 57) entry 4 May 1945, pp 427f.

19. Eisenhower (Note 118), pp 468ff; Walter Bedell Smith, *Meine drei Jahre in Moskau*, Hamburg: 1950, pp 23f; Truman (Note 58), pp 154ff; Milton Shulman, *Die Niederlage im Westen*, Gütersloh: 1949, p 556.

20. Dönitz, speech 1 May 1945, Appendix 7a; Schwerin, address upon taking office (Note 55) No 15, p 8, text Appendix 9.

21. Walter Bedell Smith, *General Eisenhowers sechs grosse Entscheidungen*, Berne: 1956, pp 231ff, 282ff.

22. The day after his arrival at Potsdam, Truman received the report that the first atomic bomb had been tested successfully and was therefore ready on the morning of 16 July: Truman (Note 58), p 425.

23. Wolff interview in Erich Kuby, *Das Ende des Schreckens*, Munich: 1955, pp 106ff; Rudolf Rahn, *Ruheloses Leben*, Düsseldorf: 1949, pp 282ff; Albert Kesselring, *Soldat bis zum letzten Tag*, Bonn: 1953, p 418ff; Musmanno (Note 42), pp 255f; Churchill (Note 113), pp 116ff, 209ff; Truman (Note 58), pp 116ff; Shulman (Note 132), pp 550ff.

24. Report in OKW War Diary (Note 6), pp 1662ff, also previous entry of 2 May 1945, p 1070; generally Ulrich Meister, 'Zur deutschen Kapitulation 1945' in *Zeitschrift für Ausland*, Vol XIII, Stuttgart-Cologne: 1950/51, pp 393ff.

25. Kesselring (Note 136), pp 409, 419; Kuby (Note 136), pp 109; Koller (Note 4), pp 77f; OKW War Diary (Note 6) p 1470: telex, OKW South to Jodl, 2 May 1945 (OKW files).

26. Dönitz diary, 3 May 1945 (Note 83), p 425.
27. Kesselring (Note 135), pp 420f, also Kaltenbrunner's report to Hitler 1 May 1945, 1040 hrs regarding the collapse of the Italian front: OKW War Diary (Note 6), p 1469.
28. Eisenhower (Note 118), p 468.
29. OKW War Diary, 3 May 1945, 1453 hrs (Note 6), p 1472.
30. Kesselring (Note 135), p 421. On the other hand see Keitel's telex, 3 May 1945 in which he orders fighting on 'by order of the Führer'(*sic*!). See his order, 25 February 1945, in which he ordered that military commanders who wanted to capitulate had to transfer their power of command to the Reich Commissioner for Defence, i.e. the local Gauleiter, if no other military commander was prepared to continue fighting (OKW files).
31. OKW War Diary (Note 6), p 1437; the date of signing is given here as 4 May while Kesselring (Note 135), p 421, gives it as 5 May. Similarly Fritz Freiherr von Stiegler, *Die höheren Dienststellen der Deutschen Wehrmacht 1933-1945*, IfZ Munich: 1953, p 138 (Friedr. Schulz, C-in-C Army Group G).
32. Notes, KAdm Godt (unpubl.) which he kindly made available to the author; Jodl, signal, 2 May 1945, 2100 hr to C-in-C North West (SKL files); Telex, Dönitz to Gauleiter Kaufmann, 30 April 1945, midday, see Appendix 4; OKW War Diary 2 May 1945 (Note 6), p 1470.
33. Dönitz diary, 2 May 1945 (Note 83), p 423.
34. See order 2 May 1945, 2120 hrs: OKW War Diary (Note 6), p 1669f.
35. As Notes 145, 146; Schwerin, 'Kapitulation' (Note 55) No 15, p 8.
36. Eisenhower (Note 118), p 469.
37. Shulman (Note 132), pp 555f; Montgomery (Note 112), p 344.
38. In Holland Seyss-Inquart probably negotiated with General Smith about foodstuffs and the supply of essential goods for the occupied territory, but 'skilfully' and 'strictly' declined to capitulate – under the influence of Generaloberst Blaskowitz: report by Blaskowitz, 30 April 1945, sent 0129 hrs (SKL files); telex, von Blaskowitz, 2 May 1945 to OKW South, forwarding the report to Jodl on 3 May 1945 (OKW files); Eisenhower (Note 118), pp 458f; Smith (Note 134), pp 251ff; OKW War Diary, 1 May 1945 (Note 6), p 1469; Dönitz diary, 3 May and 4 May 1945 (Note 83), pp 424f, 427.
39. Schultz (Note 26), p 70; Dönitz diary, 4 May 1945 (Note 83), pp 426f; Montgomery (Note 112), pp 344ff; in Eisenhower (Note 118), p 469 and Introduction to the publication *Germany Surrenders Unconditionally'*, *Facsimiles of the Documents*, Nat. Archives Publ. No 64-4, Washington DC: 1946, p 1 emphasises the refusal more strongly as the 'bridge'.

40. Eisenhower (Note 118), also Churchill's answer to a question in the House of Commons about what a 'partial capitulation' is (12 April 1945) Churchill, Speeches 1945, *Endsieg*, Zürich: 1950, p 255.

41. Jodl advised 'not to play the Holland and Norway trumps yet', OKW War Diary 4 May 1945 (Note 6). p 1472.

42. As Note 152; Dönitz (Note 57) p 458; Schwerin, 'Kapitulation' (Note 55), No 16, p 16, also Schwerin, *Es geschah* (Note 94), pp 370f; OKW War Diary, 4 May 1945 (Note 6), pp 1473f.

43. Facsimile report: Montgomery (Note 112), p 288; *Germany surrenders...*(Note 152), p 7, Appendix 12.

44. OKW War Diary, 5 May 1945 (Note 6), p 1475.

45. Dönitz diary, 4 May 1945 (Note 83), p 427; OKW War Diary 4 May 1945, 1400 hrs (Note 6), p 1473; Dönitz (Note 57), p 460; Order of the Day to U-boats, 4 May 1945, see Appendix 10; signal 5 May 1945, 2130 hrs that *Regenbogen* (codeword meaning, 'Scuttle boats!') had been cancelled by the cease-fire (SKL files).

46. OKW War Diary, 5 May 1945 (Note 6), pp 1474f.

47. OKW War Diary, 4 May 1945, 2300 hrs (Note 6), p 1474.

48. Dönitz diary, 4 May 1945 (Note 83), pp 426f.

49. Eisenhower (Note 118), p 470; Kesselring (Note 136), pp 411, 420f; OKW War Diary, 3 May 1945, 1453 hrs (Note 6), p 1472 (SKL files with date 4 May 1945, 1405 hrs), Eisenhower's refusal of 6 May 1945, p 1478.

50. Eisenhower (Note 118), p 470; Smith (Note 132), pp 23f, and Smith (Note 134), p 259; Dönitz diary, 6 May 1945 (Note 83), pp 430f.

51. Smith (Note 134), pp 284ff.

52. Eisenhower (Note 118), p 470.

53. Dönitz diary, 6 May 1945 (Note 83), pp 430f.

54. Smith, (Note 134), pp 260f.

55. Dönitz (Note 67) p 462; Dönitz diary, 6 May 1945 (Note 83), pp 430f; OKW War Diary, 6 May 1945 (Note 6), pp 1479ff et seq.

56. Facsimile, *Germany surrenders...* (Note 152), p 8.

57. Smith (Note 134), pp 259f.

58. Drew Middleton, 'Germans Played for Time in Rheims' in *New York Times*, 9 May 1945.

59. OKW War Diary, 6 May 1945 (Note 6), pp 1481f; Dönitz diary, 7 May 1945 (Note 83), p 432; Dönitz (Note 57), pp 463 et seq.

60. Facsimile, *Germany surrenders...* (Note 152), p 9.

61. Eisenhower (Note 118), p 471; Smith (Note 134), p 268.

62. OKW War Diary 6 May 1945 (Note 6), p 1482 (signal, 2040 hrs), *ibid* 7 May 1945, p 1482f; Dönitz diary, 7 May 1945 (Note 83), p 433.

63. Eisenhower (Note 118), p 472.

64. Facsimile, *Germany surrenders...* (Note 152), p 30.

65. Full powers for the German representatives: Facsimile, *Germany surrenders...* (Note 152), p 31, facsimile without Dönitz signature, Appendix 15b.

66. ZS No 364 (Adm. Bürkner); Archiv IfZ, Munich; Görlitz (Note 15) p 376ff; John R. Deane, *The Strange Alliance*, London: 1947, pp 173ff; Joseph W. Grigg Jr., 'Keitel is Defiant at Berlin Ritual' in *New York Times*, 10 May 1945; OKW War Diary, 8 May 1945 (Note 6), pp 1485f; Lew J. Slavin, *Die Letzten Tage des 'Dritten Reiches'*, Berlin: 1948, pp 46ff.

67. Görlitz (Note 15), p 377.

68. Facsimile, *Germany surrenders...* (Note 152), pp 32ff; see Appendix 16.

69. OKW War Diary, 9 May 1945 (Note 6), p 1487; text of the last OKW Report; *ibid*, pp 1281f; last Special Communiqué from Allied HQ, 8 May 1945, *Keesings Archiv der Gegenwart*, Vol 15/1945, p 221.

70. OKW War Diary, 13 May 1945 (Note 6), p 1493; Dönitz diary, 13 and 14 May 1945 (Note 83), pp 443ff, Appendix 24, considers the wording to be discourteous.

71. Memorandum re: 'Caretaker Reich Government' of 19 May 1945 given to the British and US heads of the Allied Control Commission at OKW on their visit the following day: Appendix 23.

72. OKW War Diary, 13 and 14 May 1945 (Note 6), pp 1494ff where all details: see Note 24.

73. Jodl's statements at situation conferences: OKW War Diary, 13 May 1945 (Note 6), p 1500.

74. Order by Jodl to Wehrmacht Command Staff South 11 May 1945 (OKW files); Jodl, situation conference, OKW War Diary, 15 May 1945 (Note 6), p 1502; Staff order from General Winter, 16 May 1945 that Secretary of State Dr Hayler (Reich Economy Ministry) and Under-Secretary Dr von Burgsdorff were to be informed of all relevant matters (both had moved into South region and were attached to OKW South). Order (OKW files), also letter from General Winter to author 20 November 1962. Report from GFM Kesselring to Eisenhower, 11 May 1945 that he had overall command and responsibility in the South, and asked for travel approval for Dr Hayler; report by General Winter about General Fangohr to Eisenhower of 12 May 1945 regarding the arrangements in the South, and report of 16 May on talks regarding these questions at US 6th Army Group (OKW files).

75. Schwerin, 'Kapitulation' (Note 55), No 18, p 16, and *Es geschah...* (Note 94), p 378.

76. Dönitz diary, 12 and esp 17 May 1945 (Note 83), pp 442, 447f; Jodl at situation conferences on 18 and 19 May 1945, OKW War Diary (Note 6) pp 1504ff, see also his statement of 15 May 1945; 'The time will come when we shall play the Russians against the Anglo-Americans', *ibid*, p 1501.

77. According to Naval Judge (ret'd) Kranzbühler in a letter to the *Frankfurter Allgemeine Zeitung*, 2 February 1963.

78. Generally, Truman memoirs, Vol 1 (Note 58) and Churchill, Vol 6, Book 2 (Note 113), also Smith (Note 134), pp 234ff, 281ff, and his *Meine drei Jahre in Moskau* (Note 132); Deane (Note 179), passim; William D. Leahy, *I Was There*, London: 1950, esp pp 342ff, or also George Fischer, 'Roosevelt-Stalin (1941)' in *Der Monat*, 3rd year 1950/1951, pp 254ff.

79. Esp Churchill (Note 113), p 414 (to the War Minister, 30 April 1945, p 416, to the Foreign Minister 14 May 1945).

80. Truman (Note 132), p 283.

81. Truman (Note 132), pp 282ff, et seq.

Chapter 4: Finis Germaniae? The Reich as a Problem of International and Constitutional Law

1. See Note 28.

2. From the gazette of the Allied Control Commission in Ernst Deuerlein, *Die Einheit Deutschlands*, Vol 1, 2nd ed., Frankfurt/Main & Berlin: 1961, pp 338ff, extract Note 26.

3. Günter Moltmann, 'Die Genesis der Unconditional Surrender Forderung' in *Wehrwissenschaftliche Rundschau*, 6th Year/1956, p 105ff, 177ff and 'Die frühe amerikanische Deutschlandplanung im Zweiten Weltkrieg' in *Vierteljahresheft für Zeitgeschichte*, Vol 5/1957, pp 241ff; Alfred Vagts, 'Unconditional Surrender vor und nach 1945' in VfZG Vol 7/1959, pp 280ff; Anne Armstrong, *Unconditional Surrender*, New Brunswick, New Jersey: 1961; Hans Dieter Viereck, *Die politische und rechtliche Bedeutung der Formel 'Bedingungslose Kapitulation Deutschlands'* (typescript, Kiel: 1952).

4. See also Lord Hankey, 'Unconditional Surrender' in *The Contemporary Review* No 1006/October 1949, pp 193ff esp p 195.

5. Philip E. Mosely, 'Die Friedenspläne der Alliierten und die Aufteilung Deutschlands' in *Europa Archiv* 5th Year (1950), pp 3040ff; Deuerlein (Note 196), pp 97ff where further literature is quoted.

6. Deuerlein (Note 196), p 36. Re the EAC *ibid* pp 60ff et seq.

7. See also John L. Snell, *Wartime Origins of the East-West Dilemma over Germany*, New Orleans: 1959, p 54.

8. A comprehensive documentation is: *Dokumentation zur deutschen Politik: Bundesmin. Für Gesamtdeustche Fragen*, previous Vol III Series/ Vol I (5 May to 31 Dec 1955) ed. Ernst Deuerlein, Bonn-Berlin 1961.

9. Mosely (Note 199), p 3039, Edward E. Stettinius, *Roosevelt and the Russians, The Yalta Conference*, Garden City, New York: 1949, pp 117ff. Leahy (Note 191), pp 353f, 356; J. F. Byrnes, *In aller Offenheit*, Frankurt/Main: n.d., pp 41ff; Robert E. Sherwood, *Roosevelt and Hopkins*, Hamburg: 1950, pp 695ff; Churchill (Note 113), p 11ff; text from Deuerlein (Note 196), pp 331ff, esp p 334, art 12a. Generally see *The Malta and Yalta Conferences 1945*, Department of State Publication 6199, Washington DC 1955.

10. Mosely (Note 199), pp 3040f.

11. Charles W. Thayer, *Die unruhigen Deutschen*, Bern: 1958, pp 37ff.

12. Also Smith (Note 132), pp 20f.

13. Rolf Stödtler, *Deutschlands Rechtslage*, Hamburg: 1948, p 27.

14. The Russian document corresponds: 'Akt o Voennoj Kapitul'acii'. Also see special communiqué from Allied HQ 8 May 1945, Appendix 21.

15. See also OKW War Diary, 7 May 1945 (Note 6), p 1482.

16. See Alfred Vagts, 'Unconditional Surrender – vor und nach 1945' in VfZG 7/1959, pp 280ff.

17. Wilhelm Grewe, *Ein Besatzungsstatut für Deutschland*, Stuttgart: 1948, p 18 (against Zinn), also Vagts (Note 210), p 288.

18. Michael Freund, 'Lebt Deutschland noch? Zur Frage des Fortbestandes des Deutschen Reiches' in *Die Gegenwart*, 9th Year/1954, p 75.

19. Street posters in the conquered German cities: author's recollection, also Slavin (Note 179), p 39.

20. Text, Deuerlein (Note 196), pp 338ff

21. Text, Deuerlein (Note 196), pp 347ff esp pp 348ff.

22. Hans Kelsen, 'The international legal status of Germany to be established upon termination of the war' in *American Journal of International Law*, Vol 38/1944 pp 689ff, and 'The legal status of Germany according to the Declaration of Berlin', *ibid*, Vol 39/1945, pp 518f.

23. From the great quantity of literature at the time of publishing, the English language versions consulted were: F. A. Mann, *The present legal status of Germany*, *ibid*, pp 277ff in *Jahrbuch für intl. und ausl.öffentliches Recht*, 1948/49; and Kelsen (Note 216).

24. Theodor Maunz, Deutsches Staatsrecht 12th edition, Munich/Berlin: 1961, pp 17f.

25. After 1989 the problem became even more insoluble. At the 'reunification' of 'Germany', the Eastern part was found to lack the provinces of West and East Prussia, Pomerania and Silesia. These had been annexed and settled by Byelorussia and Poland in the interim. The point was made by Herr Lüdde-Neurath in his Foreword to the Second Edition that parts of the German Reich as it existed at 31 December 1937 could not be hived off legally to other nations without the express will of the people of the Third Reich either by plebiscite or a treaty signed by their representatives. This after all had been the root cause of the Second World War when Germany could not obtain a treaty from Poland for Danzig and the Corridor. Since the Government of the Third Reich was abolished on 23 May 1945, and no treaty had been signed by then with the Hitler or Dönitz Government, it would appear that in international law these four provinces remain today annexed German territory. Because it lacks continuity with the Third Reich and is not elected by the electorate of the entire Reich as it existed at 31 December 1937, it would also appear to be the case that the present Federal German Government cannot remedy any aspect of the situation in international law though it may pretend to have the capacity (Tr).

26. Also Karl Dieter Erdmann, 'Die Regierung Dönitz' in Gesch, *In Wisenschaft und Unterricht*, Vol 14/1963, pp 359ff.

Index